Triangle of Success

The SAAN Story

By Albert D. Cohen

The SAAN Story © 2002 Albert D. Cohen

Park Mark Publishing Co.
1370 Sony Place
Winnipeg, Manitoba R3C 3C3

Printed in Canada

National Library of Canada Cataloguing in Publication Data

Cohen, Albert D. (Albert Diamond), 1914–
    The triangle of success

    Cover title: The story of Saan.
    Includes index.
    ISBN 0–9731101–0–4

    1. Cohen, Albert D. (Albert Diamond), 1914– 2. Saan Stores
Ltd.--History.   3. Gendis Inc.--History.   4.
Businessmen--Canada--Biography.   5. Cohen family.   6. Department
stores--Canada--History.   I. Title.   II. Title: Story of Saan.
HF5465.C34s22 2002   381'.141'06571   C2002-910656-7

--

Contents

PROLOGUE

My first book, **The Entrepreneurs**, was published by McClelland and Stewart in 1985. It went on to win the 1985 National Business Book Award Certificate of Merit. This was awarded by The Financial Times of Canada and Coopers & Lybrand.

This book is the second book of a trilogy and the result of the unexpected success of my first one. I was pleasantly surprised when I was asked to write a sequel to it. Since my initial foray into writing has been out of print for over a decade, and there appears to still be public interest in my experiences, I am incorporating updates on many of the events described in the 1985 book. I was encouraged by the many letters that I received from readers who found **The Entrepreneurs** a source of inspiration. I am dedicating this book to all would-be entrepreneurs, as well as those readers who found, in my earlier book, many experiences with which they could relate.

In this sequel, I shall elaborate on my philosophy of business, especially on those relating to working with the Japanese. In many cases my comments will be informative; other will be humorous; in some others, I trust, inspirational. My travels over the many years have taken me to many countries around the world, where I encountered many different cultures and languages. These were some of the obstacles I had to overcome, in establishing my business and personal relationships.

I would like to thank, once again, my five brothers for their love, devotion and companionship over so many years, and without whose skills and good faith, much of this story would not have happened. Four have passed away since the publication of my first book. Ours was a unique relationship that could have occurred only because of the circumstance of our birth in the Point Douglas area of north end Winnipeg. Although we were born in poor financial circumstances, our parents never wavered in the vision of the success that could be built by six brothers working together as a team.

Sam passed away in Winnipeg July 28, 1988. Amongst his many legacies is his help in founding The St. Boniface General Hospital Research Foundation.

Harry passed away in Calgary July 9, 1990. Amongst his many legacies was the gift to establish The Martha Cohen Theatre.

John C. (a.k.a. Chauncey) passed away January 28, 1992 in Toronto. Amongst his legacies are his contributions to a number of research projects.

Morley passed away most recently in Montreal September 24, 2001. He will be remembered for his many contributions to worthy causes which bear his name.

The inspiration and encouragement of my wife, Irena, and my three children, Anthony, James and Anna-Lisa, who acted as a listening post to my many anecdotes, was invaluable, and I thank them for their time and understanding.

I also wish to thank Terry Smitzniuk, my personal executive secretary, for the countless hours she put into the many rewrites necessary before the book could go to the printers for publishing.

I had Allan Gould review some of the chapters and I thank him for his suggestions.

> Albert D. Cohen
>
> Winnipeg, Manitoba, Canada
> July, 2002

SAAN Stores Ltd., founded in September 1947 is celebrating its 55 year Anniversary.

Today SAAN employs permanent and part-time employees numbering 3,500 across Canada.

SAAN is a wholly-owned subsidiary of Gendis Inc. who lends its support and experience to the day to day operations at the company headquarters which serves both companies.

The executive group who are leading the Growth of SAAN (GOS) in the new millennium are:

F. Robert (Bob) Whitney

President and Chief Operating Officer
- Joined SAAN February 1997
- 35 years of extensive retail experience

Jack Sorenson

Executive Vice-Present, Finance
- Joined SAAN June 1997
- 30 years experience, financial budgeting and cash management

Norman Nowlan

Executive Vice-President, Operations
- Joined SAAN July 1997
- 30 years experience store sales and marketing

Roger Ramsay

Vice Present, Logistics and Human
    Resources
- Joined SAAN June 1997
- 28 years experience

Jim Hale

Vice-President, Information Technology
- Joined SAAN June 13, 2000
- 20 years experience

Allan Olfrey

Director of Merchandising
- Joined SAAN June 30, 1967
- 35 years experience

These are the SAAN executive team with collectively over 175 years of experience. They have the responsibility of leading SAAN to a position of prominence in the retailing business in Canada. Albert D. Cohen, founding shareholder, and his son, James, look ahead to SAAN repeating other Gendis successes.

If Gendis could take an unknown ball-point pen, Paper-Mate, in its infancy and make it the number one pen in Canada. If Gendis could take SONY in its infancy and make it the number one electronic brand in Canada.

Now it is time to take SAAN and build it to the number one chain in its particular field.

Just watch us grow !!!

SAAN Celebrates its 55th Birthday

SAAN a wholly owned subsidiary of Gendis Inc. is celebrating its 55th Birthday in September 2002. Gendis can look back with pride. SAAN is truly a Canadian company.

For the benefit of our readers, I will deal with SAAN as it is today. This history of SAAN will be related with a series of flashbacks which will take us back to the days of its creation by the two founders of SAAN back to September 1947 when the concept came about in the early post years of the Second World War.

The history of SAAN is now being brought up to date.It was first related in my earlier book entitled "The Entrepreneurs" published by McClelland and Stewart in 1985.

"The Entrepreneurs", The Story of Gendis Inc. has been sold out and is only available in public libraries and some university libraries, in particular, the Albert D. Cohen Library at the University of Manitoba. For that reason and because their seems to be an interest in the continuing history of the company, I decided to take my Paper-Mate in hand and bring up to date the Gendis saga as of the year 2002.

What better way than to continue the story where I left off in 1985.

SAAN was founded in Winnipeg, and it has remained firmly in the hands of Gendis Inc. SAAN deserves the honour role of the first story of "The Triangle of Success – The Gendis / SAAN Story".

SAAN was understandably tarnished to some extent, by it association with Metropolitan and Greenberg stores. SAAN took over the leases of 89 of those failed stores. This addition to SAAN gave the chain some benefits, but also some responsibilities. A number of the stores did not fit into the SAAN model, and became a burden, because of their operating losses. Other stores did fit the mold, however, and were quite profitable.

Head Office Gendis Inc. and SAAN Stores Ltd.

What benefited SAAN was, it had now become a national chain with representation in every province from Victoria Island to Newfoundland as well as one store in Whitehorse, Yukon, and another in Yellowknife, NWT.

Our head office in Winnipeg is centrally located in mid-Canada, and our modern distribution centre, a.k.a. the D.C., is one of the most automated distribution centres in North America.

SAAN has been profitable for the past two years, a time which has been most difficult for the merchandise and retail industry.

Commencing in 2002, SAAN has plans to expand the chain by moving into the power centres of the country. As one of the oldest surviving chains in Canada, management feels certain that this is a new era of growth, in which SAAN, with the backing of Gendis Inc., will again resume the growth it showed in its early years.

We have the support of our suppliers, not only in Canada, but also in the countries who are our suppliers in the Far East. There is no question that they appreciate the integrity with which they were treated in the recent difficult years.

> Albert D. Cohen
> Chairman, President
> and Chief Executive Officer

The New SAAN Plan

Wednesday, April 10, 2002 was a watershed day. It marked the opening of our new format store in Mission, B.C. on that day.

This store is a model of the new store strategy that SAAN will follow in the future growth of the chain. The store is 10,000 square feet in size, which we find is the exact dimension to accommodate our plan. The store carries ladies, men's and children's wear and shoes for the family.

The aisles are spacious to allow easy access to the various displays of merchandise. The signage is attractive and visible to attract customers to the section in which they are interested.

It was after many months of planning and meetings with the experts in merchandising and operations that this new format for SAAN was developed. The enthusiastic acceptance of our new format by the hundreds of customers who have shopped at Mission since our opening gives us confidence that our new format will develop not only to service our thousands of customers who usually shop at SAAN but will serve to attract many new customers who will find values in the SAAN merchandise for the first time.

We know that we have the best quality, most attractive styles and friendly and helpful attendants who are there to assist and make shopping easier for the SAAN customer.

We have scheduled up to ten new stores for 2002 and have confirmed leases for five new openings at this time.

Our aim is to open across Canada at least 100 new SAAN Stores in the new format. Please watch for these new openings in your areas and we welcome any comments, critical and we hope complimentary over the next few years.

Thank you for the existing and we hope new customers over the coming years.

Robert (Bob) Whitney
President and Chief Operating Officer

Harry, Morley, Joe, Alexander, Albert, Chauncey, and Sam Cohen.

Flashback: Columbus Cohen and his Descendants

My grandfather, Frank Cohen, who was born in Krosnotovka, Russia, near Kiev, immigrated to Canada in 1890. How did he wind up in Winnipeg? He had saved a small amount of money, and when the pogroms began, he decided to move to the New World. When he met with an agent who was selling trips on the CPR, he had no idea where to go; he had no friends or relatives in Canada. He was asked how much money he had, and when he replied, the agent declared, "That'll buy you a ticket as far as Winnipeg, which with its French population, is known as the Paris of the west." And that, according to family legend, is how we and eventually General Distributors ended up in the prairies of Canada. Frank's three brothers, equally by chance, landed in the United States.

In due time after his arrival in 1890, Frank Cohen worked and saved money by doing many menial jobs. Through the offices of the Jewish Colonization Society, run by Baron de Hirsch, he brought over, as was the custom, his wife Feiga, whose maiden name was Oxenendler, together with his three sons, Alexander, Jake and Nate, and daughter, Vera. This did not occur until 1901, when my father, Alexander, was seventeen years of age.

By that time, my grandfather had established somewhat of a reputation as an entrepreneur amongst the Jewish community of Winnipeg. He was given the nickname of "Columbus" Cohen, as he was considered one of the early Jewish pioneers in the city who had discovered Winnipeg. The demographics of the time suggest the truth of the matter; there were but four Jews in the city in 1881; by the time of the next census, twenty years later, there were 1,514. By 1911, the number had shot up nearly seven-fold to over 10,000, and nearly double that by 1931.

My grandfather was a tall, imposing figure, with a full white beard. He always had a twinkle in his eyes and many stories to tell. Soon the Jewish community considered him as one of the wise men, and people often came to seek his advice. He had bought two rather shabby houses, improved them, and then moved his family into the one located at 450 King Street. He also had acquired the adjoining land and put up a building that became known as the "Cohen Block".

My mother, Bereka Riva Diamond, possessed some great inner strength. Married at the age of twenty to Alexander Cohen, some six years older, on May 10, 1910, she was the youngest of three sisters. They and two brothers were brought to Canada in the early 1900s by Samuel Diamond, an Orthodox Jew well-versed in the Talmud and Hebrew teachings.

In the first decade of our parents' marriage, six sons were born. John, and finally Chauncey, as he would eventually become known, was born in 1911. His nickname came about by running together his given name John C., which evolved into Chauncey. Harry was born in 1913; I was born a year later, in 1914; Morley was born in 1916; Samuel in 1919; and Joseph in 1921. My mother finally despaired of ever having a daughter, and so the six Cohen brothers, together with my parents, made up the Cohen family unit.

My grandfather had arranged the purchase of a small, divided house on Lorne Avenue, in Point Douglas, in the Winnipeg North End. As a family of eight, we lived in one side of the house known as 86 1/2 Lorne Avenue, while another family of eight by the name of Cohen (no relation), who later changed their name to Garland, lived in the other half. Each ground floor consisted of a kitchen, a dining room and a parlour. An almost vertical stairway led to a second floor, consisting of a small room with a toilet facility and two bedrooms. There were two beds in each of the bedrooms. Four brothers, of which I was one, slept in one bedroom, and the two eldest brothers slept, together with my parents, in the forward bedroom, overlooking the street.

There was a trap door from a pantry on the first floor, with a ladder that led down to the cold cellar. It had an earthen floor and was used to store vegetables, jars of preserves, homemade wine and other perishables. Under the floor were the water pipes, unprotected and uncovered, which often froze in the frigid Winnipeg winters. To overcome this, usually a trickle of water was left to run from the open tap in the kitchen. Often, in spite of this, the water would freeze in the pipes, and before they cracked it was necessary to crawl under the kitchen floor from the cellar and thaw them out with a plumber's blowtorch.

The house itself was unheated, except for the kitchen stove. The stove also served to heat water, the only source of hot water. A wash tub served as a bath, and every Saturday was bath day for all six children. My mother cooked all the meals, washed all the clothes and mended them, as they were handed down from one brother to the next. I remember how ashamed I was, going to school wearing large patches on the seat of my pants, where invariably they wore out. How different from today's poor-chic, in which young people take pride in wearing patches on their jeans!

From my earliest days, I was conscious of the financial condition of my family and was determined to try and alleviate it to the best of my ability, and to help out at home. My mother, impelled by the dire circumstances in which she found herself, was the great driving force in prompting me to find some means of helping the family. My father, a gentle soul, more inclined to scholarly learning and music (he played the violin quite credibly, having never taken a lesson but learning by ear), struggled to make a living, without too much success.

His first job was lowly; he cleaned the streetcars in the car barn in North Winnipeg. Soon after, he bought a horse and wagon and became a drayman. He would compete with many others, meeting the incoming trains at the CPR station and delivering trunks and baggage to different parts of the city.

At the age of ten, I sold newspapers with my brother, Morley. Our route was Logan Avenue between Main Street and Sherbrooke. We bought ten newspapers for 25 cents and hawked them at 5 cents each. This was our routine after school hours. At the age of eleven, after school, I graduated to working at a drug store, delivering parcels for a payment of 10 cents each. Between the ages of twelve and fifteen, I worked for Gladstone and Karr Shoe Stores, delivering shoes by bicycle. Finally, I learned enough about shoes that, at the age of fifteen, I became a shoe salesman at Gladstone and Karr, earning $5.00 for Saturday employment from 9:00 am to 10:00 p.m. Whenever I earned any money, it was all brought home to help the family finances.

If one were to ask me where was the turning point and major first milestone of my eventual business career, I would have to begin in the year 1930, at the start of the Great Depression, when I had just turned 15 years of age.

Into the World of Finance

In order to pinpoint the beginnings of what was to become the remarkable success story of Gendis Inc., I must relate my father's early involvement in the world of business.

In the 1920s, there was a cigar factory on Sutherland Avenue near Main Street. Father obtained a job there rolling cigars, and I have an early memory of visiting him. The foreman, who had taken a liking to him, suggested he buy a few boxes of cigars and call on hotels, pool halls and other likely places after working hours, to make a few extra dollars. This proved successful. Soon after, father developed some entrepreneurial spirit by writing to a Quebec biscuit manufacturer and adding their product to his line. Grandfather had rented a portion of the Cohen Block to a candy manufacturer named Joe Schwartz, and soon father was selling his line of chocolate bars, manufactured by Progress Candy Co.

A period of relative prosperity in the middle and late twenties seemed to be happening. Father began to expand his horizons by packing a trunk and a couple of suitcases with products, taking the train to such faraway places as The Pas, Flin Flon, many towns of northern Saskatchewan, and to Kenora, Fort William and Port Arthur in northern Ontario. This was long before the latter two were merged into Thunder Bay. I remember the occasions of joy at home when the mail would arrive after father had been away for a couple of weeks. Besides a letter detailing his experiences, invariably there would be a postal money order for $100 or $200. Mother would rejoice, and we shared her happiness in paying off the accumulated bills at the corner grocery store, the milkman and the baker. Often, the neighbours had been good enough to loan some money until the order arrived and they were paid back our borrowing.

Life went on like this until the year 1930, when the financial markets crashed around the world. Suddenly, father could not generate any sales to speak of. Although we always had paid the interest on the $500 mortgage on our half of the house, we never paid anything towards the principal. Now we could not even pay the interest, and we were threatened with losing even the modest quarters at 86 1/2 Lorne Avenue. After completing grade nine, at the age of fifteen, I decided to leave school and help out the family.

During summer holidays, I worked at the Hudson's Bay Company in the basement women's shoe department for $15 per week. Having reached my full height of six feet, I was able to pass myself off as being eighteen years of age. This job lasted for a short period of time. I then worked for Gladstone and Karr, this time as a shoe salesman, for $12 per week. Although the salary was not high, I was able to keep my three younger brothers, who were still in school, in shoes and socks, as well as buying the odd pair of shoes for mother.

The following year I returned to school, at mother's insistence, and finished grade ten at St. John's Technical High School. Even at that age, I was consciously entrepreneurial. When I discovered that the gym teacher wanted to buy runners for the class, I told him that I could get "a deal" for him. I contacted Gladstone and Karr and made the purchase of the dozens of pairs of gym shoes - at a commission of 10 cents a pair for myself.

It was late June, 1931, when mother suggested that I take a few boxes of chocolate bars and call on stores in our neighbourhood. I took five boxes under my arm and visited stores along fifteen blocks of Lorne Avenue, Austin Street and then down Euclid to Sutherland. I sold these five boxes for a profit of $1.25. If I want to set a time for the birth of my career as a salesman, I guess that is as good a date as any. It started as a request for some spending money, and I found that I could produce a profit in selling. That was all the inspiration I needed, even though it was a little tougher the second time around.

My father's eyesight was poor. He was quite shortsighted, and it was necessary for him to wear thick prescription glasses. He had never driven a car, but often was given rides by travelers who owned cars and enjoyed his company. He was a great storyteller, and often took his violin along with him, or sometimes played violins which some of the storeowners owned. I suspect that probably he often was glad to escape the constant financial problems at home and welcomed the chance to get away.

I had made up my mind that I would not return to high school, and told my mother that I wished to buy a car, so that I could act as a driver for father and assist him in selling his line of wares. I had never been a brilliant scholar, usually because I was working at night, whether as a messenger boy or salesman. I believe that, after the initial parental objection, my mother welcomed the idea of another breadwinner in the family. But where was the money to come from to buy a car?

An opportunity arose when a cousin of father's, Charlie Cohen, who had an interest in a body repair shop, advised that Trader's Finance had taken possession of a number of 1930 Model A sedans from a Ford dealer in Moose Jaw who had gone into bankruptcy. These were new cars and were to go on sale for $600 each, with a down payment of $200. This seemed an insurmountable problem.

Mother came to the rescue. By scrimping and saving, quietly she had accumulated $100 of capital, which she had put aside for an emergency. She then approached a friend of hers named Shifra, and borrowed $100 from her. It was then arranged through Trader's Finance to pay $30 per month for eighteen months to finance the balance of $400. Delivery of the car was arranged through Dominion Motors. It was a proud day when I drove the car to 86 1/2 Lorne Avenue. I was the envy of some of my friends as an owner of an automobile, but now I had the responsibility of meeting monthly payments, and the words of my Uncle Nate, my father's brother, still rang in my ears: "Albert," he said, "a car is like a woman. It's not the first cost, but the upkeep for which you are now responsible."

I went to work with enthusiasm. My father and I arranged to fill the car with chocolate bars. We removed the back seat of the new Model A. We started off every Monday morning to call on variety, general stores and drug stores throughout Manitoba.

We had laid out some routes. The first trip was to Portage La Prairie, then through the Riding Mountains, on to Brandon, returning to Winnipeg via Carman, a trip of about 300 miles. The following week we traveled north to Riverton and back to Winnipeg via the inter-lake area. We would just go into the towns and call on the stores. Even the smallest town had at least one general store and a Chinese restaurant.

I was proud that our name on the counter chequebooks was shown as A. Cohen and Son. Chauncey and Harry, the two oldest, were still living at home and working at the Furby Theatre and later, in the film exchange at $12 a week as revisers of the films. In 1932, we thought of anglicizing our name to A. Conroy and Son. But when we came across a merchant with the name of Conway, who wanted to know what part of England we were from, I decided to stick with our own name. At least that told us, and the world, who we were.

The first winter was a trying one. We decided that rather than spend $30 for a car heater, we would try to do without. It was a bitterly cold winter, and we would cover our shivering knees with an old coat and a blanket. The roads were poor, and often we would have to travel through farmers' fields when the roads were covered by huge snowdrifts. In the spring, the muddy roads were even worse; often we got stuck so badly, a farmer had to pull the Model A out of the gumbo with a team of horses. We usually would pay for the help with a box of chocolate bars and the farmers were very kind and cooperative. Somehow we managed to pay for our wares and scraped together a few dollars to make the car payments and a bare living.

Over a period of time, as we traveled and called on merchants throughout Manitoba, I took over more and more of the selling and promotion of our products. The chocolate bars cost us 55 cents for a box of twenty-four, and we sold them for 80 cents. The stores would then sell them for 5 cents each and get back $1.20.

The local manufacturer would wrap bars in names that I had printed for us. Sometimes I would have the same bar under two or three different names, to make more of a variety, names such as Lucky Jim, Sweet Jane, and other names I chose. Storekeepers would often say, "I'll take a box of this and a box of that," leading to a doubling and even tripling of sales. My father had a classic complaint, "I don't *like* those names you choose! They have no meaning!" "What names would you choose?" I would ask. "Why," he would reply, "I would choose a name like Oh Henry or Sweet Marie!" I offered no comment and accepted the criticism.

Of interest, may be how the way of selling could be used to advantage. Tapper Candy Co. supplied us with chocolate bars. One of the most successful was a box where the chocolate bars had a wrapper which when removed, would show the price to pay. The price was 1 cent to 5 cents each. It was surprising how well these sold particularly in pool halls and Chinese cafes. I decided to use this principal with the Stratford Pens and priced them at 1 cent to 69 cents. Of course there was only one pen at 1 cent, two at 5 cents and the total would work out to the equivalent and average of 50 cents for each pen.

This method of merchandising increased the sales by tripling because of the chance involved. It's a long cry from what the governments do today with the various lotteries held throughout the country. It is amazing that the human spirit is still enticed by the chance of winning a prize whether it is a pen for 1 cent or a prize of a million dollars.

The following incident happened to me a few years later after the family had moved to Calgary. It was many years later when Gendis was successful I was interviewed by the *Reader's Digest* magazine. This reprint from the July 1997 edition is self explanatory:

> There was one particular customer in a small town with whom I got along very well. Every month or six weeks, he'd buy ten boxes of chocolates from me. This store was off the highway, access was a mud road. One day, when it was raining, I was thinking of turning around and going back to the gravel road when I met him on the road. He was heading out of town, and I asked, "Do you need anything?" "My daughter is tending the store," he replied; "You can sell her ten boxes of chocolate bars." When I arrived at their tiny store, I said to his daughter, "I saw your father and he said you could buy ten boxes of chocolate bars. But you look pretty low; maybe you should buy 20!" She agreed, and paid me for them.

> A month later, I went back to the store on my regular rounds. The merchant looked at me and declared, "I had told you that you could sell my daughter ten boxes of chocolate bars, but you sold her 20. I feel that I can't trust you. Therefore, *I won't do business with you anymore.*" I apologized, but he never bought anything from me again regardless of how many times I called on him.

> *That incident taught me a lesson I have never forgotten - just working hard all the time isn't enough. When you give your word, you are on your honour. If somebody trusts you in business, you must never break your word.*

We Move to Calgary, Alberta

In the summer of 1932, brother Harry, who worked for Warner Bros. in the film exchange, had an opportunity of transferring to Calgary, and Chauncey joined him a few months later to work for Columbia Pictures. They had both been able to contribute somewhat to help out at home. Once they departed for Calgary, this assistance was not available, and the burden of looking after the family fell more and more on my shoulders.

The Depression deepened, and with it, sales became harder and harder to come by. Morley, Sam and Joe were still in school. Father became depressed and probably could see no solution to our difficulties. The straw that finally broke the camel's back was a trip that I made with father to Dauphin, then up north to Arran, Saskatchewan. We spent the night there with Isaac Diamond, my mother's brother who was a cattle buyer. The next day, we traveled back to Russell, Manitoba, and by the end of the week, returned to Winnipeg. Our total sales for a week's work were less than $40, hardly enough to pay for the expenses. It was then that I determined to try and escape to Calgary like my older brothers, and get away from the never-ending problems of trying to eke out an existence in Winnipeg.

It was February 28, 1934, when I managed to borrow $25 for a train ticket and some extra money. The weather when I left Winnipeg was a frigid thirty below, Fahrenheit. When I arrived in Calgary, it was during one of that city's famous Chinooks, caused by warm winds from the Pacific coming over the Rocky Mountains. It was about thirty *above!* People were walking about without coats, and it seemed as if I had arrived in a new world. I was met at the train by my brothers, and moved into the Sills Apartments on Fourteenth Avenue.

The first thing they asked me was, "Do you have any money?" I said, "I have $5.00". "Good," they said, "we can go to Jimmy's on 8th Avenue and 1st Street and have lunch." Would you believe it today, for 25 cents, we had soup, chicken croquettes, apple pie and coffee.

I soon realized that, although the climate was much warmer than Winnipeg, jobs were just as elusive. Try as I might, I could find no employment in the film exchanges, where Chauncey and Harry worked, or in any department or shoe store. Aside from the odd temporary employment, I had much time on my hands. I used my extra time to find a much larger, furnished place, the Lorraine Apartments on Twelfth Avenue, for $30 a month.

In the summer of 1934, my brother Morley decided not to go back to school and began to drive for father, taking over where I had left off. They soon decided to come out to see Calgary, and one fine day they moved in with us. Because I could not find a job, I decided that we would try selling chocolate bars again, as well as some products that we bought from National Jewelry of Winnipeg, who imported a number of items from Europe. The best known of these were the Kaschie "Bullet" lighters. The Bullet was a highly desirable lighter, which many farmers in western Canada praised for its sturdiness and reliability. We paid $3 a dozen, selling them for $4. They were, in turn, sold for 50 cents each, enabling the storekeepers to gross $6. We were, of course, one of *many* middlemen selling the product; there was no exclusiveness back then for the product.

On our first trip travelling north to Red Deer, I was amazed at the difference in the size of the towns and the ease of doing business. It seemed like paradise, compared to Manitoba. There was more mixed farming in Alberta, and people were far more prosperous. And with Winnipeg representing 80 per cent of the population of Manitoba, that province's towns were comparably small. To this day, I joke that the two greatest exports of Manitoba are the famous Goldeye fish and entrepreneurs. If someone can be reasonably successful in Manitoba, he can be successful almost anywhere in the world. It is a very, very tough market.

After a couple of months of travelling throughout Alberta, we were convinced that the family would fare much better in Calgary. In a meeting, the brothers decided that we should have Mother, and the two younger brothers who were still in school, move from Winnipeg. Harry arranged through a real estate broker to rent a home at 1230 Westmount Boulevard for $30 per month. This two-storey house facing the Bow River seemed like heaven compared to 86 1/2 Lorne Avenue, back in Winnipeg. The house had no furniture, but Harry said not to worry. He would make arrangements to buy furniture on time payment through Barney and Abe Groberman, who had a furniture store on 8th Avenue east.

Leaving Morley in Calgary, father and I drove our new 1934 Ford Sedan Delivery back to Winnipeg. In the short few months that father had been in Calgary, and once I saw the trade possibilities in Alberta, I had arranged, with the help of Harry, to trade our 1930 Ford at Maclin Motors for a delivery sedan. It had a door at the back that would facilitate the delivery of merchandise to our country accounts.

It was a happy day when we packed our few belongings in Winnipeg, and though we were crowded, with three adults, as well as two youngsters who lay on some blankets in the rear of the vehicle, we made our trek back to Calgary. Mother was thrilled with our new home, and without delay set about putting things in order.

We established our first business address in the basement, storing the merchandise on the preserve shelves, and our counter chequebooks now carried a new name and address:

> Confection Distributors and Agencies
>
> 1230 Westmount Blvd.
>
> Calgary, Alberta.

Into Direct Imports

Sam and Joe were enrolled in school. Morley worked for a short time with A. Paperny, a magazine distributor, for the sum of $6 per week, until I finally persuaded him to come and join us, telling him I would buy a car and assign a territory to him. This he agreed to, and a used 1934 Dodge Sedan Delivery was bought. It cost $600, but we had built up a bit of financial respectability at the time; we were doing business on a cash basis, and were able to finance the car and make payments to the bank. The addition of Morley's territory meant that more room for merchandise was needed, so it was decided to move from the basement of the house to the garage at the rear. Some shelves were built, and because there was no electricity in the garage (originally it had been a stable), I had to use candles when working there.

To my surprise, when returning from a trip, I found that Sam had run a wire from a connection in the house to the garage, and now I had the convenience of electricity! What luxury! The sense of wealth was limited, however; there was no such thing as saving, or anything to plow back into our tiny business. It was a matter of paying our existing bills, and paying some of the old bills we had left back in Winnipeg. It would often be discouraging; whenever I'd manage to save a few hundred dollars, my mother would use it to pay our outstanding debts. On the other hand, a profound sense of responsibility to pay all bills was very strongly instilled in us by her.

In 1936, I decided to take a trip to Toronto and Montreal, to enlarge on the lines we were selling and hunt for new ones. Chocolate bars were bulky. As we were delivering from the cars, I learned my first important lesson in merchandising: try to sell small items for high added value. Kaschie lighters and flints were an example of that. These sold well at good prices, yet did not take up much room in the car.

In Montreal, I became acquainted with Arnold Fisher of Belgo Canadian Mfg. Co. He, in turn, introduced me to Elias Brothers and Reich Brothers, importers of various products from the USA, Europe and the Far East. Because I made sure that we always paid our bills on time, I was able to give our two candy companies in Winnipeg as credit references. Earlier, before we moved to Calgary, a second candy company owned by Sol Tapper known as Tapper Candy Company had become a supplier to us. In due time, the merchandise I ordered arrived in Calgary. It sold well, and to eliminate the middleman's profit, I was determined to become a direct importer, instead of buying merchandise from importers in the East.

One of the fast moving items I brought in from Elias Brothers was the Stratford pen - a combination pen on one end and pencil on the other which we bought for $3 a dozen and sold for $4. Usually, the importer eliminated any address of the manufacturer, so that a customer could not contact the factory direct. But on one of the cartons I was able to make out the address, "Salz Brothers, Carlstadt, NJ." I therefore wrote the factory, enclosing our order for twelve gross pens, and at the same time giving them some credit references. To my delight, the order was accepted, and I was able to buy the pens at a far better price. *This was my first experience in direct importing,* and it showed me the importance of being able to purchase on a direct basis from the manufacturer.

A second item that I was able to import direct was a line of dust goggles, which were used by farmers to protect their eyes when threshing wheat. We bought these for $4.00 a dozen. After duty and taxes, they landed at $6.00 per dozen. We in turn sold them for $9.00 per dozen. The retailer sold the dust goggles for $1.25 a pair. I had bought these originally through Butler Bros. of Minneapolis. Because the address of the manufacturer was shown on the box as "Columbia Protektosite, Columbus, Ohio," I wrote them directly and was now able to give Salz Bros. of Carlstadt, New Jersey, as a credit reference. By importing these two items from the manufacturers, I discovered I could sell them to department stores and other wholesalers in quantity and still make a reasonable profit.

As the decade of the thirties was coming to a close, considerable progress had been made in the improvement of the family fortune. It was in 1938 that nineteen year old Sam decided to leave Central Collegiate Institute upon completing grade twelve. This meant purchasing a third car, and assigning a territory to him.

Father made only the occasional trip with one of the sons. I was kept busy, looking after the accounts, ordering merchandise, and making new contacts for direct importation. Joe, the youngest brother, was still in school. Chauncey and Harry, the two eldest brothers, had moved up to more lucrative positions in the film exchange, the former a manager at Columbia Pictures, the latter a manager at Warner Brothers.

In the early spring of 1939, I traded in my car for a new 1939 Dodge sedan. In order to save the freight cost of bringing the car from the factory in Windsor, Ontario, I arranged to pick it up there. I was planning a buying trip to Montreal and later New York, so this seemed to be a logical way to take delivery.

After encountering some springtime prairie blizzards, it took me about nine days to arrive back to Calgary after spending 4 days in Winnipeg, putting on close to 4,000 miles in re-routing through the U.S. The 1939 Dodge was never the same after the shock of that trip.

On my return, I found that brother Harry had rented premises for the family enterprise at 130, 9th Avenue West. This was across from the Pallisser Hotel, a most desirable location. Eventually we bought the property. Today this is part of the property upon which the Pan-Canadian Building is now located. Roy Beaver, who operated a restaurant across from the Palliser Hotel, had leased Harry an empty store next to his location. Beaver had heard that someone was interested in opening a coffee shop which would compete with him, and he wanted to forestall this possibility. As Harry used to stop there for coffee every evening, he was aware of this and suggested that Beaver lease the store to us. Beaver was paying $50 a month, and he agreed to lease the premises to us to protect his restaurant from possible competition.

This move was a major step. It meant a telephone, a few fixtures, some office furniture and the hiring of the first outside employee. Sales were about $300 per week per man, so with four brothers on the road, the average was a little over $1,000. We worked on a profit of about 20 per cent of the gross, but most of the money went into automobiles and living expenses. We were still all bachelors living together with our parents. We differed from most other salesmen, in that our day was never merely nine to five; we would call on restaurants and pool halls until eight, nine and ten at night.

As confectionery had gradually been phased out and replaced to a large extent by direct import items and products supplied by other importers, I decided that it was time again to change the company name. The name chosen was General Distributors Company. It seemed to me that this name was broad enough to encompass whatever new products might be obtained in future years.

Finally, on April 1, 1939, a sign above the new premises "General Distributors Co." was posted up for all to see. The first employee was an efficient young lady named Clara Litchinsky, who served as receptionist, typist and all-around Girl Friday for the newly formed company. It

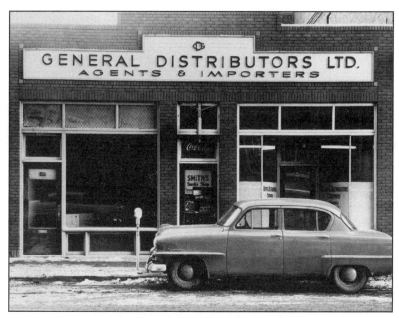

*General Distributors Ltd. first office at 130 – 9th Avenue West,
Calgary, Alberta.*

was established as a partnership, with father as president, and equal shares
for each of the brothers, except for Chauncey and Harry, who were still
employed in the Calgary Film Exchange.

Joe, the youngest of the brothers, joined the company in the summer of
1940, after finishing grade twelve. From the earliest time that he was given
a territory, he showed a natural aptitude for salesmanship. Consistently,
he brought in the best weekly sales.

The province of Alberta was now divided into four territories. Morley
was assigned the Peace River and territories running east of Edmonton
as far as Saskatoon. Sam worked the territories east of Calgary and north
to Stettler, Camrose and Hanna, while Joe covered the territory south of
Calgary to Lethbridge and southwestern Alberta. I spent less and less
time on the road, concentrating on the accounting and correspondence,
and looking for new lines. I still spent about three days a week working
the territory north of Calgary to Red Deer, Rocky Mountain House and
as far as Edmonton.

Thus, by the end of the thirties, we had become established as a sales
wholesalers for a number of brands. None were exclusive agencies, and

it was a very competitive business. However, the hard times of the early thirties were now behind us.

Father was now semi-retired. The two elder brothers were gainfully employed in the film exchange, and the other four brothers were busy travelling on the road, selling merchandise on a cash basis. Slowly, a base was being established, and, unknowingly, we were being schooled the hard way in the fine art of salesmanship, by actual experience in the field.

If the experience of travelling Manitoba in the early years of the Depression gave me my undergraduate degree, the years I spent on the road in Alberta was where I received my Master's. One thing I was very much aware of was this: until General Distributors was successful in obtaining a product that was in demand, and on an exclusive distribution basis, it would be very difficult to be any different from the many other agents or wholesalers in Canada.

IT WOULD BE MANY YEARS LATER BEFORE WE WERE
ABLE TO NEGOTIATE OUR FIRST EXCLUSIVE AGENCY
~ PAPER-MATE BALLPOINT PENS ~

During the Depression Thirties, the kernel of what eventually matured into Gendis Inc. was born. Through necessity and not by choice, I became the assistant to my father in his endeavors to provide for the family. The time spent travelling on the road with father from 1931 to 1934 in Manitoba was probably the most severe apprenticeship a salesman could have. After our family moved to Calgary in 1934, the involvement of the three younger brothers, Morley, Sam and Joe, became important, so that by the end of the decade a partnership was born.

Because the family, through necessity, had always been closely-knit, it never occurred to me as the founder of the company to take a larger percentage of the shares than any of the younger members as they joined the company. In respect to father, he was allocated 30 per cent of the stock and each of the four brothers received 17.5 per cent.

As of December, 1940, the total worth of the company was $8,639. Sales for that year totaled $40,658. By the end of the decade, the problem of the Cohen family earning enough money to maintain a fair standard of living had been solved. The name General Distributors Company was registered provincially, and the future growth of this company lay ahead.

Making Time with Watches

In the 1940s, four of the brothers were married: Sam to Leatrice Diamond of Fort William (a distant cousin); Harry to Martha Block of Calgary; Joe to Frances Belzberg of Calgary; and Chauncey to Gwen O'Sullivan of Vancouver. As we took on new responsibilities, it became more and more obvious that if the family were to remain in business together, the venture would have to expand, so that larger salaries could be accommodated. At this time, we were basically peddlers, selling things out of our cars. We sold merchandise, paid for it and brought in more, carrying very little inventory.

In 1940, as the Second World War moved from the first phase, what was known as the "Phony War," to the Battle of Britain in 1941, the Canadian economy began to develop on a larger scale. Because Great Britain had to look to the New World for men and supplies, her factories ravaged by the savage bombings of Nazi Germany, more and more products came from Canada to supply the war effort. Even in far-off Alberta, supplies became short, so sales to the country merchants became easier, providing the merchandise was available.

On one of my buying trips to Montreal, I was introduced to a new supplier, Morris Wein. Wein was a watch importer located in the same building as Arnold Fisher of Belgo Canadian Company. Fisher made the introduction and suggested that perhaps we could handle Wein's line of wrist watches imported from Switzerland. The Wein brothers had been successful in escaping from Germany; one brother had established himself in Geneva and was exporting watches via Portugal, another neutral country, to Canada. These were shockproof, waterproof watches of good Swiss quality. Wein had no representation in western Canada, and he persuaded me, even though we had never sold any watches before, to buy 36 of his Swiss imported watches.

When they arrived in Calgary, Joe took them out on his trip through the southern territory. On his first stop in Okotoks, only twenty miles south of Calgary, he sold the entire stock to Wentworth's, a general store. That first experiment convinced me that watches were an item that we should carry in our line. They fitted perfectly into the proven formula: *small items that did not take up much space, which had high dollar value.* The Stratford pens and watches became two very important lines in our varied and growing list of products.

Now the challenge became how to import watches on a direct basis. The answer came by chance one day when I was in Toronto, and while walking down Bay, near Front Street. Upon looking up to the second storey of the corner building, I saw a sign that read, "Swiss Board for the Development of Trade." I decided to call on this office and see if they could help in the direct importation of watches. I asked for the man in charge and met a Mr. Zeurrer. When I explained what I was looking for, at first he could not help. Suddenly, he declared, "Just a minute." He went out and returned with an assorted tray of about twenty watches. These were samples of a shipment that were in bond and had not been claimed by the importer. The manufacturer was Rodana Watch Co. of Bienne, Switzerland. Correspondence began with Mr. Hans Baumgartner, the owner of Rodana, and an order was placed for 2,000 watches.

It was not known whether these watches would ever arrive in Calgary, as they would have to travel by train to Lisbon, Portugal, and then by ship to Montreal, eventually arriving in bond to Calgary. And the Atlantic Ocean was not terribly safe at this point of the war. A letter of credit had been posted to ensure the factory that, on arrival, the watches would be cleared by customs and payment would be made.

Although I had made these arrangements, I wondered if the watches would indeed make it to western Canada. I had volunteered to join the Royal Canadian Navy in 1942, and it was in the spring of 1943 that I received my call to report for duty aboard HMCS Tecumseh, then HMCS Strathcona, in Halifax. Morley had preceded me in joining the Royal Canadian Air Force. Chauncey was to follow, joining the RCAF in 1944, as was Joe, who entered the Royal Canadian Navy Voluntary Reserve.

Therefore, it was left to Sam to keep General Distributors alive. Harry and Sam had received their calls and were exempted from service. It was then that Harry decided to leave Warner Brothers, where he had advanced to the position of manager of the Calgary branch. He felt it was more important to keep the family business on an even keel, while awaiting the return of the brothers.

The watch business had proven to be the mainstay of General Distributors at this time. The first shipment was sold before they were ever cleared from bond. They had landed for about $12.00 apiece, and we sold them for $17.00 each. Because watches were in short supply and the fact that I had been able to negotiate a quota for imports became very important for those times.

Sam was young and aggressive and he was able to establish excellent contacts with the American Army Post Exchanges and Salvation Army canteens, which became substantial customers for the company's wares. The American Post Exchanges were set up for troops who were building the Alaska Highway. These PX stores were established on the bases where the US soldiers were stationed. They carried a large variety of merchandise, usually at prices far below what they sold for in ordinary retail stores. The PX stores had many lines of watches, but none of the sturdy, waterproof, shockproof watches that we were able to supply.

The post exchanges were strung out from Edmonton into Alaska. The difficulties of calling on these far-flung outposts were overcome when Sam was able to secure a first priority pass to travel to Alaska on US Armed Forces planes. Some of the orders he was able to obtain were very substantial. To fill them, Harry made trips to Montreal, Toronto and Winnipeg, purchasing most of the watches from other importers. This was the first big breakthrough in increasing General Distributors sales to almost $1 million in 1945.

Between them, Sam and Harry not only kept the company alive, but also saw it through a very difficult period. In these same years, our first branch office was established in Vancouver, BC, and a larger office was opened in the New Hargrave Building, in Winnipeg, leading to a total of fifteen employees.

At the end of the war, when the brothers returned to Calgary, it was decided that Joe and Chauncey would manage the Vancouver office, Morley and I would take care of Winnipeg, and Harry and Sam would look after the Calgary office.

At first it was decided that each office would be autonomous. This did not work out, because it was found that one office would be buying a product that another had overstocked. The only way we could survive was to have one office designated as head office to co-ordinate all the buying. Winnipeg, it was decided, would be headquarters, and I took over as general manager of the company.

In the aftermath of the war, merchandise was very scarce, as the factories were slow to gear down from a war economy and take care of the pent-up demand for consumer goods. It was decided that we would have to open a branch in Toronto, if there was any chance to acquire an exclusive agency for Canada-wide sales of an exclusive product.

Fortunately, we had connections in Toronto, where sales had been made to United Cigar Stores Ltd., a chain of retail tobacco and sundry outlets. As well, Peoples Credit Jewelers, a Toronto-based retail jewelry chain were buying some of our import products. It was rather unusual for a Winnipeg company at that time to be able to sell to such large accounts in Toronto. We succeeded through perseverance and personal contacts with Bill Dawson, the president of United Cigar Stores, and Frank Gerstein, the founder and president of Peoples Credit jewelers. They recognized a young entrepreneur, and I suppose they got a kick out of listening to me, and decided that if they could help me, they would. I think they recognized things in me that I didn't know I had. After all, I was selling from the Canadian West to the East, which was contrary to what anyone ever did at that time.

A major opportunity came in the spring of 1947. I used to go down to the Merchandise Mart building in Chicago, wandering through, looking for possible lines to carry. I spotted an item of interest and was told that the only way I could get any of the product was to make contact with Royal China Company of Sebring, Ohio. I met Bea Miller, the widow of the founder and gained her confidence. I ended up purchasing three carloads of Blue Willow dinnerware sets, which were in very short supply. I was successful in selling a carload to Peoples Credit Jewelers, another to Cassidy's, both of Toronto, and the third was sold to Marshall Wells of Winnipeg. The profits generated from these three sales, roughly $5,000 from each car-load, provided the necessary capital to open a branch in Toronto.

We were on our way to become a national Canadian company with four offices across Canada. Our head office remained in Winnipeg with branches in Toronto, Calgary and Vancouver.

The Reynolds Pen -
Losing a Sale but Keeping a Friend

One other event occurred in the latter part of the forties that with time proved to be very important in the future fortunes of General Distributors.

As an example of how the post-war market was starved for consumer products, an entrepreneur by the name of Milton Reynolds of Chicago, on a trip to Mexico City, had purchased several ballpoint pens. Back in 1940, Ladislao Biro, a Hungarian who had emigrated to Argentina, patented the first, workable ball-point pen. The problem was to fit a tiny steel ball into a brass or steel tube, which had a metal nose cone at the end. There had to be just enough room at the junction, so that where the steel ball rotated, it would allow just enough ink to be picked up by the ball, to allow it to act in the same manner as a fountain pen, which was the common way of writing at the time. It was the Biro pen which Reynolds had spotted. He was impressed with this new form of writing instrument, and decided to manufacture an American version. Raw materials were still very hard to come by, but being in the aluminum fabricating business and having a stock of aluminum, he was successful in producing the first US ball-point pen.

He arranged to have the pen packaged in a plastic display tube, and priced it to retail at $12.50, sold exclusively through Gimbel's Department Store in New York. Full-page advertisements in the New York newspapers, and saturation radio advertising, sparked a buying spree that can only be likened to the Cabbage Patch Doll craze of the 1983 Christmas season. Customers lined up to buy the pens, purchasing as many as a dozen at a time. The pen became a sensation, and as I was in New York when this promotion broke, I lined up and bought a few.

I then got in touch with the factory, where I was informed that the vice-president in charge of sales was in New York. I was interested in trying to get an exclusive for Canada, as I was still on the lookout for an exclusive product for General Distributors.

When I met with this individual, I asked him about the possibility of an exclusive arrangement for Canada. He indicated that what they had in mind was granting not one exclusive, but a number of them, each to do with a certain classification of trade, such as jewelry stores, tobacco trade, drug stores, etc. The export price he quoted was $6.50 per pen. I figured it would cost an additional 50 per cent, because of duty, sales and excise taxes. This would mean a landed price, including transportation, of about $10.00 per pen.

I stopped in Toronto to call on Bill Dawson, the president of United Cigar Stores Ltd., to show him the pen, and get his reaction as to whether he would be interested in selling it in his chain of stores.

When I arrived at Dawson's office at the appointed hour, I was greeted warmly. When I related to Bill the enthusiastic reaction at Gimbel's Department Store, he was quite amazed. Although he had read the news reports of the overwhelming response, hearing me confirming the fact first-hand really impressed him. I showed him the two pens, and when he tried them, they wrote reasonably well. I told Dawson that I had the opportunity of obtaining the line for the tobacco trade, and asked him if he would be interested in placing an order.

After some deliberation and further discussion, he called in his buyer, Watson, and asked him to write up an order for 1,200 Reynolds pens at $12.00 each. This was an order for $14,400, which at the time represented a very large order for General Distributors.

When I returned to the Royal York Hotel where I was staying, I was having some second thoughts. I had intended to see Dawson just to get a reaction to the pen, and here I had quite a large order. The question was, having lined up Dawson, should I now proceed to try and make a deal with Reynolds?

Deep down, I knew that the fragmented type of approach of splitting up the distributorships to different segments of the retail trade could not possibly work. What was to prevent the Reynolds distributor appointed to sell to the stationery or drug wholesalers from approaching the tobacco trade as well? I decided if I was going to work out anything with Reynolds, I would have to speak to Milton Reynolds himself, and try to make him see my point of view. If he would agree to consider one agent for Canada, then I was prepared to meet him in Chicago and work out an arrangement.

When I finally reached Reynolds, I told him of my thoughts and suggested I would come to Chicago to discuss this in greater detail. His answer was, "Albert, save yourself the trouble. We have inquiries from Europe, Canada, and all over the world. I don't have the time to meet with you. Besides, we have made up our mind that this is the way we are going to market the Reynolds pen in Canada. If you want to get on the bandwagon and make a lot of money, tie up the pen for the tobacco trade in your country." With that final statement, he ended our conversation.

Instinctively, I knew that this method of merchandising was wrong. Moreover, as I used the pen, I became more and more disenchanted with it. It did not write smoothly. The ball seated in the tip of the refill had a tendency to slide, instead of rolling the ink onto the paper, the ink smeared and blotted.

The next day I went back to see Dawson and told him of my decision.

"Bill," I said, "I want to turn back the order you gave me for the Reynolds pen."

"Why?" he asked me.

"I've thought it over, and I have come to the conclusion that I would not be doing you or our company any good. I don't feel that the pen, in spite of all the publicity it's getting, is good value."

With that, I turned back his order to him. I also informed him that he could contact Reynolds directly, if he wished to. I pointed out that we were going to make $2.00 profit per pen, so he could bring these into Canada at a cost of $ 10.00, instead of the $12.00 I had quoted him.

At the same time I said, "Bill, I would recommend that you forget the Reynolds pen, because you will probably have a lot of grief if you decide to sell them in your stores."

Bill thanked me and tore up the order. "Albert," he said, "in my experience, this is the *first time* a salesman has turned back a signed order to me. I'll make it up to you some time in the future."

With that, we shook hands. When I left Bill Dawson's office, I breathed a sigh of relief. I was certain that if I had gone through with the deal and delivered the pens to United Cigar Stores, I probably would have lost a friend, as well as a good customer.

The pen was soon the butt of comedian jokes, in which it was described as *"the only pen that could make perfect copies without making an original!"* Angry customers, taking advantage of Gimbel's unconditional guarantee, mailed back many hundreds of the Reynolds pens for refunds, often accompanied with laundry and dry cleaning bills. Due to the changes in atmospheric pressure on airplanes at that time, ink would often pour out of the refill and unto the clothes of the angry users. I was not interested in seeing our company involved in selling a product that we could not back up with our usual guarantee.

Within a year of its spectacular launching and seeming success, the Reynolds pen became a crashing failure. Because of the faults I had seen in the product, customers kept returning the pens to Gimbel's, and other outlets, for cash refunds. Reynolds went out of business, but not before he made millions of dollars with his venture into the ball-point pen business. And by 1950, these new kind of pens were selling for $1.00 each and some at even lower prices. They were of the same quality as the Gimbel's-backed pen. No better, perhaps, but certainly no worse.

So ended the first introduction of the ballpoint pen to America. The experience I had gained, however, served me exceedingly well a few years later, when I encountered Paper-Mate.

By the close of the 1940s, there was a greater maturity to General Distributors. Whereas I had thought that the company would suffer when I joined the Navy, it prospered instead, indicating solid strength. Chauncey, after discharge from the RCAF, joined the company in 1945. Both he and Harry were given equal shares in the company, so that all six brothers were in the venture with equal shares.

Although the head office was in Winnipeg, our branches in Calgary, Vancouver and Toronto showed that we could now offer any manufacturer national distribution. By 1950, we not only had the eight SAAN stores, but we were firmly established as an import house, importing and representing such firms as Sunware Inc. of New York, manufacturers of Rayex Sunglasses, and Century Glasscraft Inc. of Chicago, manufacturers of decorative glassware.

We had established contacts by correspondence in Italy, France, Switzerland, England, Japan and Hong Kong, and we were importing various and sundry items from these countries. However, that one exclusive item that would make our company into a truly national one had not been found. It was not until the decade of the 1950s that Paper-Mate and SONY were to become the keys to the future, explosive growth of General Distributors.

During these years, one of the things I instilled in everyone was that if you take too much money out of your business, you won't have any business left. My brothers used to joke that when they came in off the road at the end of the week, I would pick them up by the heels and shake them: any money that stuck in their pockets was their salary. This was another way of saying that everything was turned in, and only a few dollars were doled out for spending money.

My principle was: *your first responsibility was to pay your suppliers. Only then could you take your living expenses from the profits.* So there was very little in the way of salary, right into, and through, the 1950s.

In the meantime, as illustrated by the balance sheet of December 31, 1949, the net worth of our company had grown to $39,627. Total sales were $605,903, which, together with SAAN sales of $474,636, gave a grand total of $1,080,539 for the year ending on the last day of the decade. Hardly millionaires - but we had broken at least the barrier of one million dollars in sales, less than a dozen years after General Distributors was born.

The Paper-Mate Story

There are two kinds of luck in this world: the blind, Irish type, where you win the sweepstakes, and the other side of that type, where you can be killed crossing the street.

I am a firm believer that one creates one's own luck. That type of luck is made by a person who has built up a background of knowledge, so that he can take advantage of opportunity when it knocks. That type of luck does not happen by accident. First of all, the basic intelligence has to be there. It is honed by experience, studying, reading, and an intense, concentrated interest in the chosen field of the individual. There were two situations of that type of luck which presented themselves in the early and middle fifties, and they became the seeds of the ultimate success of General Distributors.

By January, 1950, General Distributors had become established as a true import company. From Sheffield, England, we were importing a line of knives and cutlery. Washington Potteries Ltd., with head office in London, was a supplier of earthenware. Bayard & Cie, of Paris, France, was a supplier of alarm clocks. Etna Watch Co. of Geneva, Switzerland, and Rodana Watch SA, were suppliers of watches and watch movements. Frank Corsi SA, of Milan, Italy, was a supplier of earthenware novelties. These were some of our principal suppliers, but there were many more. We had even hired two watchmakers in Winnipeg, who were assembling watches under the Gendis brand, a contraction of our company name and the eventual title of our firm. The reason for that was because the duty was lower on imported movements than completed watches. Yet I was still hunting for that one, special product that would be exclusively ours.

For all our expanding market, we had occasional difficulties. During the first year of what would be the most eventful decade in the history of our company, our line of credit was exceeded at our bank. We were even threatened with having all our cheques returned as NSF, unless we promptly reduced our borrowings to the established $25,000 line of credit. Here, the traditional kind of luck came through. My brother,

Harry, during the postwar years, had attempted to build a theatre chain, and had acquired four movie houses, two in Winnipeg and two in Calgary. Although they had never proven very profitable because the business was on the wane with television coming in, still we were fortunate to be able to obtain a mortgage on the Valour Theatre property in Winnipeg. This $50,000 tided us over until we were able to generate sales, reduce inventory, and bring us back to a reasonable ratio of debt to equity to satisfy our bankers.

Then, one cold, January day in 1952, opportunity came knocking at our door. The result was our first exclusive item - and one which was soon to become a renowned brand name around the world: Paper-Mate.

One of the contacts I had made in New York was with a firm known as National Silver Inc. They were one of the largest importers and wholesalers in the US, with a big and glossy showroom on lower Fifth Avenue. After the initial contact was made, General Distributors imported a number of their items for sale in Canada.

Late in January, 1952, I received a phone call from National Silver's representative in Seattle, who had approached brother Joe in Vancouver to sell some products. Joe had referred him to me, as the buyer for the company. Evidently, his territory included western Canada, as well as the north-western states. I arranged to see the wares which he had on display in a sample room in the Royal Alexandra Hotel.

It was a bitterly cold evening when I met with the man at the Royal Alexandra Hotel. I decided to place an order for about $1,000, not that we needed the products, but out of sympathy for the salesman, remembering how tough it was to write business in Manitoba.

As he was writing up this order, I noticed the ballpoint pen he was using was quite different from anything that I had ever seen before. I asked if I could examine it.

This pen had a black plastic barrel with a gold coloured, laminated top. It possessed an innovative plunger which, when pushed, clicked because of a metal latch spring, which either projected or retracted the writing point, locking it in place. Upon unscrewing the barrel from the top, I found that it had a brass ink refill, which, like other ballpoint pens on the market, could be replaced by a new one when dry.

The origin of the name was evident from the two interlocking hearts on the metal clip, which I assumed was suggesting the marriage of ink to paper. The ink was quick drying, and I was amazed to find that as rapidly as one wrote, there was no blotting or smearing, the ink was absorbed immediately by the paper.

Being responsible for the buying for the company, and always on the lookout for new, original items, I was immediately impressed by the features of this new pen. Opportunity was knocking ever so softly at that moment, and had I not been alert to the sound, she would have swiftly passed me by. My radar was always alert for that one unique product for General Distributors, and I had searched practically the world over for that elusive item. Could it be here in Winnipeg, on my own doorstep, where I would find the exclusive item I was looking for?

I asked the National Silver salesman for the sample pen, but he did not want to part with it. The only information he could give me was that the pen was manufactured in Los Angeles, that it was a very hot seller, and that the brand was Paper-Mate. I saw that I would have to trace the address on my own if I wished to contact the manufacturer.

General Distributors had, as noted earlier, some previous experience with pens. The first one we had imported was the Stratford pen of Carlstadt, New Jersey, and after the war, I had my narrow escape from the eventually disastrous Reynolds pen. Being in the general import business, at that time we were importing a low-priced ballpoint pen from a supplier in New York, who sent me the address of the manufacturer of the Paper-Mate pen:

> The Frawley Corporation
>
> 8790 Hays Street
>
> Culver City, California

Once I had the address, I immediately wrote the company to see if their line was available for Canada. In due time, I received a formal reply, with some free samples enclosed. These included their standard pen and their deluxe pen, which was the one that had piqued my interest a few weeks earlier. The letter was signed by George Lewis, vice-president. A price list was enclosed, and knowing the duty and other tax factors involved in importing the pen, I worked out a landed cost. I estimated that the standard pen would sell in Canada for $1.49, and the deluxe pen for $1.98.

I decided to see if there would be an interest in the product, before I investigated the matter any further. Therefore I had Hy Lee, our city salesman, call on Syd Florence, the stationery buyer of the T. Eaton Co. in Winnipeg.

The report that I got back was discouraging. According to Lee, he was told by the buyer that the pen was over-priced: they were selling a well-known brand, the Waterman ballpoint pen, for $1.00, and sales were only just fair. An unknown, unadvertised brand, therefore, would be of no interest to Eaton's.

I was disappointed in the reaction. However, I carried the deluxe Paper-Mate pen around with me everywhere. The more I used it, the more convinced I became that there *should* be a market for this product. I was taken by its innovative features: the retractable tip, the fast-drying ink, and its new, unique design.

I happened to meet with Bill Dawson, the president of United Cigar Stores, who was on one of his periodic trips through western Canada. I showed him the Paper-Mate pen I was carrying with me, and I asked him if he knew it. To my surprise, he was fully acquainted with the pen, and was aware that it was making an impact on the trade on the West Coast of the US. He had seen it in New York, where Goldsmith's, a large stationer located in Wall Street, had brought some in, and were featuring this new product.

I then told Dawson that I had contacted the factory and was trying to get the agency for Canada. Dawson declared, "Albert, I haven't forgotten the Reynolds episode. Following your good advice, we never did buy that pen. If you obtain the Paper-Mate agency, contact me and I'll give you an order and prominent window display space in all of our stores across Canada."

I thanked Dawson. With this confirmation of the viability of the product, I decided that the next day I would phone the factory. If the line was still available for Canada, I thought of flying to Los Angeles to meet with the principals of the Frawley Corporation.

I placed the call the next day, and when the operator came on the phone, I asked to speak to George Lewis, the vice-president, as this was the only name I knew connected with the company. I was told that he was out of the city, but if I wished to, I could speak with a Mr. Eddie Ettinger, who was involved in sales. When Ettinger came on the line, and I found out later that the first question he asked of his operator was whether the call was collect, because if it was, he was not going to accept it. Fortunately, it was not as I would never call collect if I was trying to impress the person I was calling. I introduced myself and told him the purpose of my call. The first question he asked me was, "Where's Winnipeg?"

I told him of our four offices located in Toronto, Winnipeg, Calgary and Vancouver. I added, "We are a family of six brothers, and we have a brother managing each office, for instant communication." This intrigued him. I then asked if the Paper-Mate pen distribution was still available for Canada. His answer was, "Come down here. I'll make a reservation for you at the Beverly Wilshire Hotel, I'll show you our plant, and then we can talk about it."

I made my arrangements and arrived at the Beverly Wilshire on the evening that Ettinger had made my reservation. There was a message to call his home. His wife, Shirley, was expecting my call, and she told me that the factory was working a night shift and to call her husband there.

When I met Ettinger for the first time that evening at 8790 Hays Street in Culver City, I was impressed by his appearance: he was the prototype of the exuberant, aggressive salesman, described best by the cliché "tall, dark and handsome." It was quickly apparent that he lived, breathed and talked Paper-Mate day and night. It was his all consuming passion, and as he showed me around the plant, working the graveyard shift, spewing out pens by the thousands, I was soon caught up in his enthusiasm. Surely, I thought to myself, if the factory has to work day and night to satisfy the demand, then **this** is an agency that I **must** secure for the Canadian market! *This could be the exclusive item for which I had been scouring the world.*

The challenge was now to convince the Frawley Corporation that we were the right company to represent them in Canada. Time was of the essence, as well; other potential agents in Canada had discovered Paper-Mate, and a few months had passed since I had first seen the pen. As a matter of fact, the factory had already shipped a few sample orders to Grand and Toy in Canada, but, fortunately for us, no exclusive arrangements had been made.

To my mind, the perfect item I was looking for had to have certain qualifications. First, it should be small in size, so that no large warehouses were required to store and service it. Second, it should have a good dollar value; in other words, a retail cost of anywhere from $1.00 to $5.00. Third, the item should be of good quality, with some unique features to make it desirable to the public. Paper-Mate seemed to meet all three necessary requirements.

The next morning, I met Ettinger at his office. He seemed to be receptive to my approach for the exclusive rights to distribute Paper-Mate in Canada. He told me, however, that Pat Frawley, the owner, was the only one that could make the ultimate decision. He was in San Francisco and was expected back in two or three days. Ettinger, being ever the salesman, suggested that in order to impress Frawley, I should sign an order for a quantity of Paper-Mate pens and refills.

"Albert," he added, "write a cheque payable to the company for your order. When I hand your order and cheque to Frawley, this will help me clinch getting his okay for you."

After some deliberation, I decided to take Ettinger's advice. I gave him the cheque and the order, which amounted to $20,000, with these words: "Eddie, we'd both better be right, or else we'd better start running south to Mexico, because I'll have five brothers chasing me with shotguns."

I was spending every day at the factory, getting the feel of the Paper-Mate operation. I studied their newspaper advertising campaign and their method of selling. I also realized that I had to make arrangements to have my cheque honoured, so I called Mr. Russell at the Bank of Nova Scotia to tell him what I had done. I also sent some sample pens to brother Joe in Vancouver, and asked him to call on some of his accounts to book orders on the commitment I had made.

Later that week, Pat Frawley returned from San Francisco, and I had the chance to meet him for the first time. When I was introduced to him, I was immediately taken by his youth. He was only twenty-eight, with red hair, dark, penetrating eyes and a ready grin. He was about five feet ten inches tall, well built, with a ruddy, freckled complexion, the heritage of an Irish father and a Nicaraguan mother.

"Eddie has told me a lot about you," he warmly greeted me. "So, you want to take on Paper-Mate for Canada?"

This was a positive statement, so I responded in like fashion. "Pat, I *know* we can do a great job for you in Canada. As a family of six brothers in business together, located in four different cities across the country, we will give you the kind of cross Canada distribution that *no one else could do* in so short a time!"

Frawley's reply to my enthusiasm was more critical: "I have your Dun and Bradstreet report, which shows that you have only a net worth of about $35,000. I don't think you have the necessary finances, even if you *are* successful in the marketing of Paper-Mate."

I assured Frawley that the financing would be available. Then, using the strategy that Ettinger had suggested, I handed him the order, together with the cheque for Paper-Mate.

Ettinger, with whom I had become very friendly in the few days we had spent together, then spoke up to the boss: "Look, Patrick, I have a lot of confidence in Albert. With six brothers working together, how can you miss? Let's give General Distributors the agency for Canada, and try it for one year. If they don't pay their bills, you can charge it against the bonus you owe me."

This was a very fine gesture on the part of Ettinger, and I felt very grateful to him for the confidence he showed in me. I found out in following years just how perceptive he was in many of the business judgments he was to make.

"Okay Albert," Frawley laughed, putting his arm around my shoulder, "we have a deal. We won't forget Canada in our thinking and planning."

On many occasions afterwards, when I was appointed to the board of Paper-Mate, and sat in on many of the important meetings and decisions as we were finalizing them, I would declare, *"And don't forget Canada."* This generally brought on a laugh, and Ettinger would chime in with one of his favorite expressions, which was "Shoot the rabbit." This was his rallying cry for "Come on gang, let's get out there and get the job done."

In spite of the Reynolds fiasco, which left the market in a very chaotic state, most of the pen manufacturers attempted to manufacture a pen on the ballpoint principle that would write satisfactorily. All the well-known brand names, such as Shaeffer, Waterman and Eversharp, had tried, but been unsuccessful in mastering the necessary technology. Indeed, the latter, one of the leading brands in pens, had staked their reputation on producing a ballpoint that they guaranteed and claimed was perfect. It was priced at a whopping $15, and millions of dollars were spent on advertising its qualities. The pen proved to be a dismal failure that did not stand up to its claims, and Eversharp's stock went into a decline from which the company never recovered.

Other top brand names had similar experiences, but only Parker, with their very successful Parker 51 fountain pen, ridiculed the ballpoint principle, claiming they would never manufacture such a pen. With the success of Paper-Mate, they had to eat their words. They soon witnessed the fast decline of the fountain pen, and had to produce a ballpoint under the Parker brand.

On July 31, 1952, a two-page contract, loosely drawn on Frawley Corporation stationery, was signed between the two companies. This gave us the exclusive distribution rights for Canada, but the contract could be cancelled by either party on only thirty days notice. It was now up to us to produce the necessary sales to satisfy Frawley.

The opportunity was there, but could we take advantage of it? **I was determined that wc would!**

At last, we had an exclusive item in the booming ballpoint pen business! We introduced Paper-Mate pens to the Canadian market, and in a very short time, it became the number one seller, generating over $2-million in sales - and gaining me the nickname of "Mr. Paper-Mate" in many areas of the country. These were profitable sales, which helped establish the growth and future success of General Distributors Ltd. – a.k.a. Gendis, as we were now identified in all our contractual documentation.

Eddie Ettinger

Patrick J. Frawley
Founder, President, CEO
PaperMate Pen Company

A Brief History of the Pen That Would Help Make Us Successful

The next couple of weeks were spent in studying the product, its features and methods of generating sales for a product that was generally held in disrepute. I made many calls with Eddie Ettinger on large drug store chains and stationery stores, and soon was able to create a plan that I believed would work for us in Canada.

During the time I spent at the factory in Culver City, I had the opportunity of getting to know the aggressive personalities who were responsible for the establishment and future success of Paper-Mate. First of all, Patrick Joseph Frawley, Jr., the guiding genius. Born in Managua, Nicaragua, the only son of an expatriate Irishman and his Nicaraguan wife, Pat inherited the good looks of his mother, together with the whirlwind drive of his father, who on emigrating to Nicaragua had successfully obtained the agencies for some of the best known American brand products.

At the age of sixteen, Pat was a salesman for his father's import-export business. At eighteen, he negotiated a $300,000 deal between Panama and U.S. Rubber, and at twenty-three, he built a flourishing export business in San Francisco, with a branch office in Manila, Philippines.

Through his business, Frawley began to sell ballpoint pens made by a Los Angeles aircraft parts manufacturer, and before long, he bought an interest in the factory. The firm was losing money, and in 1949, at the age of twenty-five, he bought out his partner for $18,000, rented a factory for $450 a month, coined the name Paper-Mate, and started manufacturing pens under that brand.

By that time, the market was flooded with cheap ballpoint pens, and bankers warned against writing cheques with them: the ink used was not fast drying, and a forger, by placing his finger on a signature, could transfer a perfect facsimile to a cheque or document!

Because the ink leaked, schools banned the use of the pens, and retailers were flooded with complaints of damaged clothing. Plane passengers discovered that a simple change in atmospheric pressure was enough to empty all the ink into a shirt or suit pocket! Frawley could not have picked a worse industry or worse timing for the purchase of his new enterprise, which he had named the Frawley Corporation.

But opportunity presented itself in the person of a Hungarian chemist by the name of Fran Seech. In a makeshift home laboratory, Seech had mixed a batch of a new ink that solved all the problems endemic to the ballpoint pen. It was the first fast-drying, non-transferable ink, and had all the properties for which the very large fountain pen manufacturers had spent millions of dollars for research and development, without success. Seech was able to demonstrate that even if one were to write on a white shirt with his formula ink, it would completely wash out in ordinary laundering, and yet the ink would remain permanent on legal documents.

After calling on all the large companies and not making any headway, Seech decided to canvass some of the smaller pen manufacturers. When Frawley's secretary told him that there was a strange, seedy-looking little man with a thick foreign accent who wanted to see him "on some important private business," Frawley was intrigued, and told her to show him in. Seech did not want to disclose to Frawley's secretary why he wanted to see him, as he was afraid of being turned away, as he had so often been when calling on the large manufacturers.

Seech was admitted to Frawley's office carrying a brown carton tied with rope. Frawley watched him with amusement, as the stranger untied the rope and removed a Mason jar filled with what appeared to be blue ink.

"Who are you?" asked the bemused, young president of Paper-Mate.

"I'm a chemist, and I've developed this fast-drying ink!"

"Where is your laboratory?" asked Frawley.

"I don't have one. I did this in the bathroom of my home," Seech replied in his broken English, soon extolling the virtues of his fast-drying ink. But because Seech had no facility to inject the ink into a refill, there was no way to demonstrate it.

"Do you want to work for me?" asked the intrigued Frawley.

"No, but I'll *sell* you the ink!"

"How much do you want?"

"There's five pounds in this jar, and I want a dollar a pound," asked the immigrant entrepreneur.

Frawley paid Seech the $5 for the jar, and promised to try it.

A few days later, Clarence Schrader, Frawley's chief engineer, saw the bottle of ink on Frawley's desk. Frawley then related his strange encounter with the Hungarian chemist, and suggested that Schrader make a small run of refills with Seech's ink.

When this was done, and the refills were inserted in the first crude Paper-Mate pens, Frawley and Schrader became very excited: *Seech's ink did everything for the ballpoint that he claimed it would!* The ink dried as fast as one could write; it didn't smear, and would not transfer itself from paper. **This was the miracle ink they had been looking for!** Seech had left his card with Frawley, but the card had been tossed into a drawer in his desk. Or had it? Had Frawley thrown it into the wastepaper basket? After a frantic search, the precious card was found.

Frawley was able to contact Seech, and asked him to meet him in his office. Both Frawley and Schrader could hardly wait for their meeting the next day, when he exuberantly told Seech that he thought his formula was good, and offered the immigrant a job with the Frawley Corporation as a chemist. Surprisingly, Seech advised Frawley that he was only interested in selling him his ink at the stated price of $1 per pound. It took a lot of talking before Frawley and Schrader were convinced that the only way they could make a deal was to buy the ink on Seech's terms. Finally, an arrangement was made: SEECH WOULD SELL HIS INK TO FRAWLEY EXCLUSIVELY. It was around this time that I first crossed paths with Frawley and Paper-Mate, which was obviously *before* they had gone national; once they had succeeded across the United States, there was no way that I and my then-small Canadian firm could have made a deal with them!

Frawley believed that the only way to sell a product properly was to go out and call on small pharmacies, stationery stores and wherever else pens were sold, but he found that pens could hardly be *given away.* His first Paper-Mate pen was crudely designed, yet he priced it to retail at $1, a premium price, because there were more attractive pens on the market selling for 25 cents each. Because he could not sell the pens, wherever the merchant would accept them, he left them there free of charge, to be paid for when sold.

Late one afternoon, after a rather fruitless day, a weary Frawley decided to stop in for coffee at a diner; there, he met Eddie Ettinger, the proprietor. Over coffee, Frawley demonstrated the quality of his new pen, even writing on Ettinger's clean white shirt, assuring him that the ink would wash out and leave no stain. The result of their meeting was that Frawley, struck by Ettinger's high-voltage personality and enthusiasm, offered him a job assisting him with marketing the Paper-Mate pen. Ettinger was full of ambition, and thought he saw opportunity beckoning, so he sold his diner and joined Frawley. They were both right in their decisions.

Another bright young man in the Frawley Corporation was an Austrian designer by the name of Walter Spatz. Frawley realized that if he was to develop and increase sales, he would have to design a pen that was more attractive. He instructed Spatz to design one that would have a retractable feature, so that the tip would not be visible. He also conceived the idea of a trademark of two hearts intertwined, to denote the marriage of ink to paper.

His instruction to Spatz was to have the new pen designed within a month. In only a week, Spatz had designed what was to become the Paper-Mate Deluxe Pen #250: it had a black barrel with a gold laminated top, which, when pressed, acted to extend or retract the ballpoint tip. It was a tremendous improvement in appearance and quality over the first Pape-Mate, and, when marketed, was a great success. His design was soon copied by manufacturers in the US and around the world.

In the fall of 1952, as the sales of Paper-Mate started to expand rapidly with the introduction of the successful deluxe pen, Frawley decided to open a factory in Puerto Rico. The American protectorate was then offering a ten-year, tax-free holiday to induce manufacturers in the United States to open branches there. Furthermore, profits would not be taxed, as long as they were not transferred to the parent company. The purpose of this off-shore plant was to supply the New York market, as well as Canada.

The most successful marketing of Paper-Mate came about when Frawley was able to persuade the Bank of America in San Francisco as to the quality of the new non-transferable, smear-proof ink. He then proceeded to run full-page advertisements in major newspapers and magazines with the new deluxe pen illustrated full-length. The eye catching heading read, "Bankers Approve the Paper-Mate Pen".

Although the initial placement of orders was done with the large wholesalers and drug store chain retailers on a guaranteed sales basis, as soon as the advertisements appeared, the demand created was beyond all expectations. The invoices were paid promptly, and all the outlets placed large repeat orders to satisfy the pent-up demand for the pens. A similar approach was made with a leading local school, and approval was obtained for the use of the Paper-Mate pen by students. The next major advertisement carried the headline "Educators Approve the Paper-Mate Pen".

To break into the New York market, probably one of the most difficult in which to introduce a new product, a radically different approach was planned, to counter the cynicism about ballpoint pens that had been left by earlier, inferior ones. It was a brilliant campaign. Twenty-two university students were trained for a period of two weeks, after which their cars were loaded with attractive Paper-Mate pen displays, each with spaces for twelve pens, but containing only six pens, leaving six empty spaces. This gave the impression that half of the display had already been sold! They were told that the pens, priced at $1.69, were to be given away free to the merchant, on the understanding that he would display the pens prominently near his cash register, use one of the pens so that he could judge its qualities for himself, and allow two window streamers to be placed on his windows announcing, *"Paper-Mate is here."*

The salesmen were then given their marching orders. Starting from their beachhead at the tip of Manhattan, in a matter of three days they had worked their way up the various avenues. It seemed to New Yorkers that overnight, the whole city had blossomed into a Paper-Mate holiday. Curiosity was aroused everywhere, and as the store salesmen became enthused with using the new pen, they all were extolling its virtues to their customers. Besides, every time they sold a pen, they made a full profit of $1.69!

Once the stores had been covered by the salesmen, full page advertisements appeared in *The New York Times* and other newspapers, as well as *Life* magazine, announcing that "Bankers Approve The Paper-Mate Pen." The result was a quick sellout by retailers, while wholesalers were deluged with requests for pens and refills. Frawley was prepared with huge stocks to supply the wholesalers, and in less than a month, the New York market had been explored, assaulted and captured. It was a campaign planned as well as any military blitz, and Paper-Mate became, in short order, the number one-selling pen in the United States.

The almost instant success of Paper-Mate over a period of less than a year generated some growing pains. Fran Seech still refused to sell his formula to Frawley or to come and work for him, despite some lucrative offers; instead, as the demand for his ink increased, he kept raising the price. As the demand increased for the pens, Seech started falling behind in his deliveries, so that a shortage developed.

Scripto Pen Inc. of Atlanta, Georgia, a competitor of Paper-Mate, started wooing Seech to join *their* company, and one day, without prior notice, it was announced that Fran Seech had signed a contract for $1-million with Scripto Pen, and joined that firm!

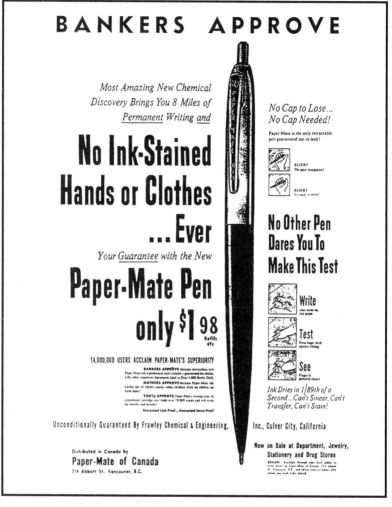

*A full-page ad in The Vancouver Sun, August 16, 1952, launching
the west-to-east Paper-Mate campaign.*

Frawley had planned for this eventuality: fortunately for him, his brother-in-law's father, Professor William Frederick Seyer, a Ph.D. in chemistry at UCLA, was the father of Frank Seyer, who worked for the Frawley Corporation as a chemist. Frank's brother, Tony, was married to Agnes Frawley, a sister of Patrick, and it was through this connection that he had first become acquainted with Paper-Mate.

The Seyers were given the task of formulating a new ink that would replace the Seech formula. They were successful, after extensive experimentation, to break down the Seech formula. The new ink, which proved to be superior in many ways, gave Frawley the independence he required. Since other chemists in other companies were working along the same lines, soon *most* pen manufacturers were extolling the virtues of their ink being "just as good" as the one used by Paper-Mate.

All this helped further establish the leadership of Paper-Mate, since the "me too" philosophy of other manufacturers acknowledged that Paper-Mate was the best.

This was a lesson I never forgot. It would serve me in good stead in future endeavours in the merchandising field. It was and is most important that when a manufacturer has a new item to introduce to the marketplace, that he observe the principle of what I call The Triangle of Success, which I shall discuss in a later chapter. This was what established Paper-Mate in a relatively short period of time as a leader in its field.

Frawley had been able to overcome the established leaders in his field, and revolutionize a technology that had been established for over a hundred years. From the early days of the New World, when scribes used the feather quill pen, to the days of the Spencer nibs, which were inserted into a holder and then dipped into an ink well, to the more recent use of the fountain pen, there had been no essential change in writing instruments. It was Frawley—an entrepreneur in the true sense of that word who put together the people and took advantage of the opportunity of using Seech's formula ink, to produce the first practical ballpoint pen, the Paper-Mate Deluxe #250, that swept around the world as a new medium of putting words on paper.

Interestingly, Gendis made no money on the pens themselves. The key to our financial success in our relationship with Pat Frawley and Paper-Mate was, of course, through the *refills.* Just like the Kodak camera: the success was not in the selling of their box camera, but in the film; there was the *real* profit; the same with Polaroid, as well. True, while one could, at that time, purchase a bottle of ink for a mere dime, the public was ready to pay for the tremendous convenience of the ballpoint refill. I decided to put the price of 69 cents on each refill which surprised Pat Frawley.

"Albert!" he once challenged me, "we charge only 49 cents! Why don't you charge 59 cents, which should cover the taxes and other costs of getting them into Canada?"

"Pat," I replied, "*you* know manufacturing, but *I* know merchandising! Once you break the 50 cent barrier, then 59 cents, even 69 cents, are the same to the public. I want to make money on these refills, and with 69 cent refills, I'll have enough left over to put into advertising, and still make a profit."

"The difference between an agent and a distributor is, as the latter, I have the right to set my own prices. I will give you what you want as the manufacturer, Pat, but I plan to pay for all advertising myself, and I want to make a net profit of 5% on the sale of Paper-Mate products."

Pat Frawley knew manufacturing well—even brilliantly, with the help of characters like Fran Seech. I knew merchandizing, and with Pat's truly new and truly improved pen, General Distributors was selling millions of refills every year in Canada. In 1955, Frawley sold his company to the Gillette Company for $15.5 million, which was a good sale at that time, and one of post-war merchandising's success stories. Of course, the new owner Gillette had its own distribution of its many products in Canada, and I knew that the time would come when Gillette would want to handle its own distribution of its new Paper-Mate division, so I continued my search for another product.

It was through my connection with Frawley, and the knowledge that I gained in bringing Paper-Mate to Canada and, soon after, working with the giant Gillette firm, that I was able to plan the future success of a quite extraordinary young company which I discovered in the early postwar years of Japan. It was called Tokyo Tsushin Kogyo Ltd., a.k.a. Totsuko, which changed the whole character of General Distributors.

General Distributors were not commission agents; we always acted in the role of importers. When making contact with a manufacturer to buy a product, it was on the basis of purchase for its own account. The merchandise was paid for (on a freight on board) F.O.B. basis. Duty, sales tax, excise tax, transportation and brokerage charges were all the responsibility of the importer. Through our company's distribution channels across the country and the close contact by the brothers in charge of each office, instant decisions could be made. The challenge we had with the exclusive Canadian arrangement with Paper-Mate gave us the opportunity we were looking for over the years.

An agent had *no* investment in the product he sold. Usually, he worked from samples supplied by the manufacturer and sent the orders in to the manufacturer for delivery. The manufacturer extended the credit terms, and assumed all risks, but controlled the account. The agent received a commission, usually anywhere from 5 to 7 per cent of the value of the orders written. Ordinarily, the agent's commission was remitted on a monthly basis.

The difference between these two methods was, of course, that the importer controlled the sale of the product, while an agent was solely controlled by the manufacturer. As a result, salesmanship was all-important for General Distributors, because in effect we were acting in the role of the manufacturer.

Almost twenty years of calling on retail merchants in western Canada had taught us the first principle of salesmanship. Primarily, it consisted of selling merchandise at a fair price, often to introduce a new product on a guaranteed sales basis. This meant that if the product did not sell well or did not prove to be of the quality promised, then we would accept a return for full credit. As we were only importers, and did not manufacture any product of our own, my buying experience was such that, when making contact with any new supplier, I had to make a value judgment, not only of the product, but also of the person with whom I was consummating a deal.

The contract signed July 31, 1952 with Pat Frawley was a loosely drawn one that could be cancelled on thirty days notice. I was therefore aware of how vulnerable we were as a distributor, and realized our relationship would be only as good as the success of our endeavours to establish Paper-Mate in Canada.

Because I had a certain marketing formula in mind, I immediately advised Harry in Calgary, Sam and Morley in Winnipeg, and Chauncey in Toronto **not** to attempt to sell Paper-Mate to any account in Canada. I wanted to apply the Frawley/Ettinger formula to the introduction of Paper-Mate in our country. I decided to introduce Paper-Mate first of all in Vancouver, and then move east, city by city.

Back in 1952, Joe was one of the best salesmen in Canada, as he was for decades after. With the samples I sent him in the early stages of my negotiations with Frawley, he had contacted some of his better accounts in the wholesale drug and stationery business. Therefore, when I stopped in Vancouver to plan our first Canadian campaign for Paper-Mate, Joe had already sold over 1,000 dozen pens and 1,500 dozen refills. We ran our first full-page newspaper advertisements in the two Vancouver dailies, and as we had good, distribution, the product was on display everywhere, and Paper-Mate was an immediate success.

I had phoned Bill Dawson of United Cigar Stores Ltd. from California, advising him that we had acquired the Paper-Mate agency for Canada. I asked him to place an order for his western stores, explaining that our campaign was to proceed from Vancouver east. This was very unusual, as all products distributed nationally had *always* been introduced in the east before coming west. However, Bill accepted my explanation and reason for the campaign, and promptly began to order Paper-Mate pens and refills for British Columbia and Alberta. The Reynolds experience we shared had not been forgotten, and I had Dawson's full confidence.

The Vancouver success was followed up in Calgary, Edmonton, Regina, Saskatoon and Winnipeg. I immediately doubled, then tripled our pen orders with the factory, and refill orders were increased accordingly.

All this required additional financing. In Winnipeg, I met with Mr. Russell, manager of the Bank of Nova Scotia. He was impressed with the Paper-Mate success, but told me that I had reached his limit, and would have to get the approval of the Toronto head office for my request for an increase in our line of credit. A meeting was arranged for me with the senior vice-president, Bob Dales.

We had not yet introduced the Paper-Mate pen in Toronto, so I took a night flight there and arrived in the early hours of the morning. Chauncey had arranged appointments with Drug Trading and National Drug, two of Canada's largest drug wholesalers. We also saw Grand and Toy, the largest stationery wholesalers, and called on the tobacco wholesalers Scales and Roberts, among others. By this time the success of Paper-Mate in the States and western Canada was well known, so we had no problems writing large orders with these accounts. We also called on Woolworth's and Kresge's, where we were similarly successful.

Metropolitan Stores' head office was located in London, Ontario, in an old, unimpressive five-storey building. George Holt, the vice-president, upon hearing my presentation, decided that they would try twelve dozen pens and six dozen refills as a test. I tried to persuade him to place an order for 144 dozen pens and refills, but he refused, saying he could always re-order if the pen was selling as well as I claimed. I was not impressed with the Metropolitan approach to merchandising, but never did I dream that within the next decade the chain would be controlled by General Distributors.

The following day, Chauncey and I met with Bob Dales of the Bank of Nova Scotia. I showed Dales the orders we had written with some of the largest wholesalers in Toronto. He was impressed, and said he wanted Sydney Frost, the president of the bank, to meet with me. When I met Mr. Frost and enthusiastically extolled the virtues of the Paper-Mate pen and the success we were enjoying in Canada, he looked at me, put his arm on my shoulder, and said, "Albert, I can see that General Distributors is in good hands. We will grant your request for an increase in your line of credit to $100,000."

In order to round out our Canadian distribution, it was necessary to open an office and warehouse in Montreal, from which to service Quebec and the Atlantic Provinces. It was early fall, and I spent about a month looking for suitable premises. Finally, I found a one-floor walkup at 7 Notre Dame Street West, in Old Montreal, just out of the financial area, a most unlikely address for our type of distribution business. However, the price was right: $125 per month.

The acquisition of the exclusive distributorship of Paper-Mate was a landmark in the development of General Distributors: within a year, we established Paper-Mate as the number one selling pen in Canada. We sold 50,000 dozen, followed by 100,000 dozen refills, within the first twelve months. And because of the prestige of the line, we found that it was easier to acquire other agencies.

American Luggage, with its Tourister brand, soon became available to us, and we were able to build additional volume with this line. Through correspondence, our imports particularly from Japan, broadened considerably, to include portable tube radios, lighters, cameras and binoculars, fishing tackle, toys of all descriptions, earthenware novelties, and many other items. I began to be aware of the growing importance of the Japanese source of supply and thought that a trip to Japan might be fruitful.

I found, however, that with the growth of Paper-Mate, I had to spend more and more time with Pat Frawley in Culver City, California. Pat was drinking heavily at that time, and I would often receive a boozy phone call in the middle of the night to come down to the Beverly Wilshire. The next day would find me on a plane. I attended many executive meetings, and found myself involved in helping to make major decisions for the company, as the merchandising experience I had acquired over the years was now available to help in the Paper-Mate marketing success.

I now realized more than ever how important it was that I met Frawley when I did, before Paper-Mate became a national marketing phenomenon across North America. As little as six months after Paper-Mate's success in New York, there is no way Frawley would have given anyone the exclusive distribution for all of Canada. By the year 1953, Paper-Mate represented 50 per cent of our sales and 75 per cent of our profits. Meanwhile, we continued to sell all the other products of our highly diversified company, without a proportionate increase in expenses.

At one time, early in our association, Frawley had offered me 2% equity in Paper-Mate for $50,000. Because that represented the total worth of our company, I hesitated in taking him up on his offer. After I saw how sales were developing, I told Pat I was ready to invest, but by then, it was too late. I had missed this golden opportunity; within a short period of time, Paper-Mate was in such demand that Frawley withdrew his offer.

On a September day in 1953, Frawley called an executive meeting in New York. As I was walking back to the hotel with him, right out of the blue he announced that he wanted to sell me a 40% interest in Paper-

Mate Eastern Inc., the shell company that handled the distribution of Paper-Mate for the eastern States. Most of the product was imported from Puerto Rico, and the sum involved was not large - only $12,500. Tom Welsh was to own 20% and Frawley 40%. There was no danger of Frawley losing control, as Welsh was the president of Paper-Mate Eastern and would always vote his shares with Frawley. I was to be appointed chairman of the board of the company. The prime purpose of Frawley not controlling Paper-Mate Eastern was to establish a fair market value for excise tax purposes. Because he did not own Gendis, our imports into Canada from Puerto Rico could be used as the base for exports to the U.S.A. In that way the excise tax rate would be established for his imports to his home market.

I told Frawley that I was willing to establish this relationship, and assured him that he could always have this stock back at the same price I paid for it. All I wanted was his assurance that General Distributors would always have the exclusive distribution of Paper-Mate in Canada. Pat assured me of that, and at the same time asked me to come to New York and join him in furthering the growth of the company. He offered me $50,000 per annum, which at the time seemed like a huge salary, vastly more than I was taking home from General Distributors.

I told Pat that I was not interested in moving to New York. I was a Canadian, and had five brothers as partners, so I could not consider his offer. Frawley laughed and told me that I should come to his lawyer's office. He understood why I would not accept his offer to move to New York, but he wanted me to own the stock. We then arranged to meet in the office of Mr. Aaron Lipper of Lipper, Shinn and Keeley, where the deal was consummated. I became the chairman of Paper-Mate Eastern Inc. and the owner of 40 per cent of the stock. All this was on the understanding that I would attend meetings but would not be involved in the day-to-day running of the company in New York.

Paper-Mate - The Betrayal
and the Resurrection

It was a few days after my return from Hawaii, early in November, 1955, that I received a phone call from Pat Frawley, they were having a problem in closing the deal with Gillette. The lawyers had found that General Distributors had registered Paper-Mate of Canada provincially in Manitoba. In order to have clear title to the name, it would be necessary to have General Distributors sign off all legal rights to Paper-Mate, so that the deal could be finalized. He advised me that the law firm of Crowell and Leibman of Chicago, who were acting on behalf of Gillette, would contact me about signing off the rights to Paper-Mate. I assured Pat that I would not be an obstacle in the conclusion of his deal, as long as he had protected our exclusive distribution rights for Canada. He gave me his personal assurance that this was the case, and as a result I asked him to have the lawyers send me the necessary papers.

When the documents arrived and were shown to our lawyer, Mark Shinbane, QC, he advised me not to sign, because we had nothing to stand on.

"How do you know that Frawley will fulfil his commitment to General Distributors?" he asked me.

"Because I have Pat Frawley's word that our interests are protected in Canada," I replied.

In spite of Shinbane's advice and fears, I sent off the papers with my signature to Chicago, so that the deal could be finalized. Besides, Frawley had arranged a meeting in New York for the following week, where I was to meet Mr. Neison Harris, the president of Toni Corporation, a wholly owned division of Gillette, who had engineered the deal with Frawley. Paper-Mate would become a division of Toni, and Frawley would continue to be the head of Paper-Mate, but under the direction of Harris. I had my doubts about Frawley working under anyone's authority and discipline, knowing his individualistic personality.

We met in a suite reserved by Harris in the Ambassador Hotel. Present were Pat Frawley, Neison Harris, Eddie Ettinger and myself. On my arrival, the three had come out of a large meeting that was still in progress. I was introduced to Harris, a legendary person who had taken a small firm named Toni, located in Minneapolis, which specialized in manufacturing ladies' home permanent kits, built it up through inspired marketing, and sold it to the Gillette Corporation for $30 million. I knew he was a person to be reckoned with. After the usual introductory and getting acquainted bantering, it did not take me long to see that I was faced with a serious problem. Without mincing any words, Harris told me that Gillette intended taking over the distribution of Paper-Mate in Canada as soon as convenient. Frawley and Ettinger sat silently as Harris was conveying this message to me.

"When do you feel it will be convenient for you?" I asked, while hiding my inner thoughts.

"Oh, I would say January 1, 1956, would be a good cut-off date," Harris replied.

"Well, I *don't* think it would be convenient for *me*, Mr. Harris! Besides, you may have bought Paper-Mate from Frawley, but you did *not* buy General Distributors Ltd! *We* own the inventory of Paper-Mate in Canada, and *we* established the product, taking it from an unknown brand to where it is today, the best-selling and best-known brand of pen in Canada. If you think I'm just going to hand over Paper-Mate on a silver platter to you without compensation, you better think again."

"We bought Paper-Mate and all the rights that go with it," Neison Harris exclaimed, rising from his chair. "I'm not going to get into an argument with you. If you want to talk compensation, talk to Frawley, not to me. Gillette doesn't owe you anything. If you want to discuss this further, come to Chicago for a further meeting. If you like, I'll send my private plane to Winnipeg to pick you up and fly you there."

"Why don't you fly up to Winnipeg and see our operation?" I quickly asked. "It will give you a better idea of what our company is all about. If you want to have a smooth take-over, you've got to give me some time for it. I'll cooperate with you, but *not* on a two-month notice!" My mind was already racing: *I know other pen companies down in the States, like Lindy Pen Corporation! I've built up Paper-Mate, and if I can get a year's time, I could build up another one.*

He thought for a moment and then said, "That's a good idea. I can't make it, but I'll have Joe Stampleman, the president of Gillette of Canada, and Bill Miller, my vice-president, meet you in Winnipeg."

A date for the following week was set, and Harris went back to his meeting, leaving me alone with Frawley and Ettinger.

"Pat," I said, "This isn't as you assured me last week. You promised you would protect our interests in Canada. Upon your word, I signed the papers as you had asked me to do."

"Well, Al, you know what these big corporations are like," Frawley shrugged. "When I tried to tell them about the terrific job you had done in Canada, they said they have their own distribution and didn't need anyone else to do the job for them.

"You know, Al," he continued, "as long as you are a distributor or an agent, you will always be vulnerable to a take-over or sell-out. You should get into manufacturing yourself."

"It's okay for **you** to say that," I bitterly protested. "You are getting over $15 million for Paper-Mate. You can afford to give that sort of advice, but you are leaving me high and dry." Paper-Mate was probably worth only about $8 million, but the profits were all in Puerto Rico, which suited Gillette. They could use the profits out of Puerto Rico in another subsidiary without bringing the profits back to the U.S.A. where it would be taxed as U.S. profits.

"Just a minute," Ettinger interjected. "You haven't done badly since we gave you an exclusive for Canada."

"You keep quiet!" I turned on Eddie. "I know where your loyalty lies. I don't need any corroboration from you about this double cross."

I was furious when I left the meeting, feeling that I had been let down by business friends in whom I had put my full trust. I felt bitter and betrayed knowing how much my brothers and the company depended on Paper-Mate. Unless a solution could be found, it could mean the failure of our company. If we lost Paper-Mate, we would be just another small importer! This was our first big success, and it was disappearing, right before my eyes!

Trying to find an answer to this problem while meditating on the plane, I thought, wouldn't it be wonderful if we had one of our famous Manitoba blizzards when Miller and Stampleman arrive for our meeting? Then, they would get a sense of what merchandising is like in this northern clime!

When I brought the brothers up to date on the events that had occurred in New York, they were deeply concerned as to how we would cope with the situation. It was clear that we could *not* look for any help from Frawley. It seemed evident that with the swiftness of events, and the huge sum of money involved, that the promise made to me had become blurred in his memory.

The day of our Winnipeg meeting dawned cold, bright and clear. It did not seem as if my prayer for a Red River blizzard was going to be answered. Miller arrived from Chicago with his company attorney, Charles Woodard, both wearing rather light coats! Joe Stampleman flew in from Montreal. He was the Canadian President of Gillette Corp. Stampleman was a short, stout, jovial man in his late fifties, with a round face and thick glasses. It was not long before I sensed that he was an unwilling participant in this meeting. Where I had thought he would be the one anxious to take on Paper-Mate for Canada through his Canadian organization, he voiced the opinion that selling Toni and Gillette products was more than enough to keep him busy.

This was all the opening I needed. Rather than become antagonists, I suggested to Miller and Woodard that Gillette should give us a one year contract to continue to distribute Paper-Mate in Canada. I agreed that we did not have a legal right, but there was a moral obligation for Gillette to give us a chance to obtain another agency, to make up the loss of volume when Paper-Mate was taken over. Stampleman seemed to agree, although he did not voice it, and after a few hours of negotiations, it was agreed that a further meeting was necessary which would be held in Chicago. After all, it was Neison Harris who would make the final decision.

When I drove Miller and Woodard to the airport, the temperature had dropped to thirty below, Fahrenheit. I did not learn until the following week in Chicago, that the mechanics had to use blow torches to thaw the congealed engine oil before the private plane could take off. I am sure that when Harris heard the report of that inhospitable climate in Canada, it helped him conclude that perhaps it **was** in the best interest of Paper-Mate to continue distribution through those angry Canadians in the frigid wilderness of Winnipeg. At that meeting, attended by Frawley and Stampleman, as well as Harris, Miller and Woodard, the agreement was reached, and, at least, I felt that it gave us the time necessary to plan our next move.

"Al," Frawley said to me afterwards in private, "I take my hat off to you. I never believed you could work a deal with the mighty Gillette Corporation."

"Pat," I smiled back, "the arrangement I have with them is a *better* one than I had with you! We paid cash for all our purchases from you in the

CANADA

File No. 9193-4

DEPUTY MINISTER OF NATIONAL REVENUE
CUSTOMS AND EXCISE

OTTAWA 2, March 17, 1961.

Mr. Albert D. Cohen,
President,
General Distributors Limited,
791 Notre Dame Avenue,
Winnipeg 3, Manitoba.

Dear Mr. Cohen:

I refer to our discussion on October 20th last, regarding the values for duty of Paper Mate Ball Point Pens and Refills imported from the Paper Mate Manufacturing Company of Chicago. You will recall that, during your visit, some concern was expressed that values as certified to for these products might not comply with all the present valuation provisions of the Customs Act.

In an effort to be thoroughly conversant with discounts being granted by the industry in the United States, a trade survey was conducted to determine the discounts allowed by competing manufacturers to the various levels of trade. The review has recently been concluded and a ruling has been forwarded to the exporter establishing values for duty in accordance with his prices to wholesalers in the United States, exclusive of the United States Federal Excise Tax where applicable, less a distributors' discount of 10%.

While I appreciate that you have been advised previously of the foregoing, I am writing so that you may have the assurance that the decision issued is the most favourable which may be given under the Customs law. In the circumstances, however, the Department's ruling will not be retroactive and importations cleared Customs prior to March 6, 1961, the date of issuance, may be allowed to stand as entered.

Yours faithfully,

D. Sim.

past, but Gillette agreed to give General Distributors ninety-day credit terms, and agreed to take over advertising, which I used to pay for in the past. This will help our financing immensely." *And it did!*

I found out afterwards what had happened: Joe Stampleman had told the others, "Give Cohen the one-year contract. I'm just not ready to take over. I've got enough on my plate with Toni and the other things." So I ended up with a deal that was much better than the one I had before! *They* ended up running ads for Paper-Mate, along with the Gillette program on all those baseball and hockey games, since they didn't want to spend any extra money. But it saved General Distributors spending all that money on advertising! And all of a sudden, we had gone from a near-death experience to prospering, with SONY just around the corner to put us over the top.

One lesson I learned in this exercise was how to deal with adversity. I had experienced it before, but not on such a vast scale. I could have become extremely bitter in New York, and had harsh words with Frawley and Ettinger that, once said, could not have been retracted. Instead, I was able to cope, and turn a negative situation into a positive one.

The association with Gillette proved invaluable. Their approach to business was on a much more stable and practical basis than Frawley's had been. Sales soared, and the reputation of General Distributors grew, because of our association with the Gillette Corporation. From what seemed to be a gloom-and-doom situation, all of a sudden the fortunes of the company were on a steady, upward beat. Year after year as the decade progressed, our contract was renewed. Indeed, our relationship with Gillette was wonderful, and it lasted for *seven full years* after the original gathering in the Gillette offices of Neison Harris where our contract was finalized.

The Beginnings of the SAAN Chain

When the Toronto branch opened in 1947, Chauncey moved from Vancouver to manage the branch. Sam spent some time in Toronto and was instrumental in locating the premises which we rented in the Garden Press Building on Adelaide Street, downtown. It wasn't large; perhaps 1500 square feet, and the rent was $150 a month. Sam then decided to move to Winnipeg from Calgary, together with his wife, Leatrice, and their first born. There was no way that we could all make a living in one city, and I always had the thought that we should utilize our natural resources - the brothers. We soon discovered that we had instant communication and we would speak by telephone very frequently. Usually all the brothers would call me every Friday to report on sales or other items of interest.

It was at this time that the SAAN store history began. From its very inception, it was under the umbrella of General Distributors Ltd. It was after the war, when consumer merchandise of all types was in very short supply, that the war surplus stores became established. These were outlets for the tremendous quantities of merchandise stored in various depots in Canada and the United States. Spokane, Washington, had been the staging area for the Armed Forces for the north-western states, and consequently had a great many warehouses filled with war surplus. Because the forces were being discharged, it was to be sold at the best prices obtainable.

Al Pratt, who operated a furniture store in Spokane, had good army contacts, and, through a salesman who had contacted our Vancouver office, Chauncey had bought a quantity of waterproof flashlights which sold very well.

One day, Pratt phoned Chauncey in Vancouver to ask him if he could help him out with a carload of surplus merchandise that was consigned to an account in Calgary who had not claimed it. The car was incurring demurrage charges, as it was sitting on a side railway track, and each day the cost kept mounting. The only way to stop these expenses was to deliver it to someone. Pratt offered to release the car and let us pay for the merchandise after it was sold. It was because he had had a few transactions with us which had been honoured, that he trusted us to help him out in this situation. Chauncey called Harry in Calgary, and the boxcar was released into his custody.

Once Harry had a chance to obtain some samples from the railroad car, items that service stations could use, he saw that the merchandise should be quite saleable. It was just then that Ralph Kalef came to call on Harry. Ralph had been a partner with Harold Cohen (no relation) in a firm called Smith Batteries. After a few years of struggling, the firm had become insolvent, and Ralph was looking for something to do. The thought occurred to Harry that, because this carload of merchandise contained items particularly suited to the garage trade, and because Ralph had these connections, he would be the most likely person to call on this trade and sell the carload.

A proposal was made, and in short order the merchandise was sold at a profit. Kalef earned a $500 commission for his work, and Pratt was paid for his carload. This could have been the end of the episode, but the sale produced a good profit for our company, and Harry's interest was awakened with regard to the availability of other war surplus items. Chauncey was the only one who had actually met Pratt. He had spoken to him and had been invited to come down to Spokane for a meeting. When they got together, Chauncey discovered row after row of warehouses, each one full of good, saleable merchandise. He passed this information on to Harry and myself.

As the Easter long weekend was approaching, Harry and Ralph decided to take their wives down to Spokane, a drive of about 500 miles, to meet with Pratt and see his operation. They were entertained by Pratt, and the relationship was cemented.

Both Harry and Ralph were intrigued, while in Spokane, by the war surplus stores that had been opened, and how busy they seemed to be. Because of the shortage of merchandise, women were buying parachutes to make dresses and curtains. Eisenhower jackets, which became famous in the many newsreel shots showing the general wearing one, became a teenage rage. It soon became apparent to Harry and Ralph that the West, and particularly Calgary, would be a good prospect for such a store. General Distributors had been buying war surplus merchandise, and would be a source of supply.

Camrose, Alberta 1953.

Mission, British Columbia 2002.

Therefore, in the spring of 1947, Harry and Ralph rented a rebuilt garage on 1st Street East and 7th Avenue for $75 a month. They stocked the store with a variety of merchandise, using old army tables to display the items which were piled high. Army double bunk beds, hardware and just about anything they could buy from various sources were on display. Finally, on a Saturday morning, they were ready to open the doors. The two partners ran a small advertisement in the *Calgary Herald,* announcing the opening.

The results were beyond expectations. On the first day, they rang up $2,400 in sales. The store continued to thrive, and Harry and Ralph began to realize that they were on to something very good.

It was in June, 1947, that I decided I would drive down to Los Angeles in our 1946 Buick. Morley accompanied me, and we stayed at the Santa Monica Beach Hotel. While there, I received a phone call from Harry in Calgary. He asked me to call on a war surplus wholesaler to see about purchasing some merchandise for the war surplus store that he and Kalef were operating. At the same time, he mentioned to me how well the store was doing. I was impressed, because sales were for cash, whereas the wholesale business as conducted by General Distributors was much more complicated. General Distributors had to import the merchandise and then finance the sales to the various merchants. It was a very competitive business. I thought it would be worthwhile looking into this war surplus type of operation, where it was clearly a lot easier to bring in a couple of thousand dollars in retail sales, than have to go out knocking on doors in dozens of small country towns.

When Morley and I drove back to Canada, we stopped in Vancouver to visit with Joe. Morley decided to stay in Vancouver and call on some of the B.C. accounts. Then, he flew up to Whitehorse, in the Yukon, while I drove on to Calgary.

I spent a few days in Calgary and had a chance to see the war surplus store in operation. Sales were excellent, and Ralph Kalef made the facetious remark, "Albert, you should close General Distributors and get into the retail business. General Distributors was my pride and joy, and I was briefly hurt by his remark. But I soon decided that perhaps the advice was worth following. Perhaps we could do *both*: continue distributing, and open some stores.

Mother agreed. She urged me to contact Sam and suggest to him that perhaps we could open a store in Winnipeg. Upon her recommendation, I phoned Sam and asked him to start looking for a retail store, so that on my return to Winnipeg, we could discuss this new venture.

When I arrived in Winnipeg, Sam told me that he had searched the city, and the only thing that was available was an empty store at 697 Main Street, between Higgins and Henry Avenue, on the east side of the street. We struck a deal, and agreed to pay $150 per month rent for the store, plus $50 per month for the second floor, which would be used as a storeroom.

Sam and I then visited some of the local wholesalers to buy war surplus merchandise, along with regular items, and plan for a store opening. Over lunch, we decided that we should try to find a descriptive name for our new enterprise. Looking ahead, we felt that if this store was successful, we would develop it as a chain. The store name would have to describe the type of goods which would be available; primarily war surplus merchandise.

The Army and Navy Stores Ltd. were well established in western Canada, and that name could not be used. There was already a store established in North Winnipeg operating as the War Surplus Store.

After trying a number of combinations, we came up with the following:

SURPLUS ARMY AIRFORCE NAVY

S A A N

Again, looking ahead, we believed that if we could establish the single store, or future stores, we would not lose the value of the advertising if we named it in that manner. Once war surplus merchandise was no longer available, replaced by regular imports or Canadian products, we would phase out the Surplus Army Airforce Navy title, and the word SAAN, which we had coined, would remain as the name of the store.

The foresight in evolving the name in this manner proved to be a wise decision. As the chain grew in size, we never lost the value of the dollars spent in the early years of advertising, as the original war surplus merchandise was phased out.

The company was incorporated with capital of $7,000, with ten shares issued to Father and each of the six brothers. Because SAAN did not have a credit rating, General Distributors Ltd. was the guarantor of any purchases made on its behalf.

As it was necessary for me to make a trip to eastern Canada about a week before the store was scheduled to open, I wished Sam success and left town. Mother, Father and Harry arrived from Calgary to attend the opening.

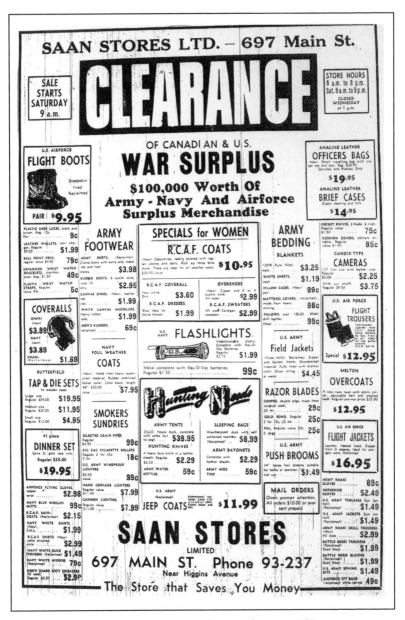

Winnipeg Free Press Ad, September 12, 1947.

On a cold day in late September, I returned to Winnipeg from Toronto. Leaving my bags at the apartment, I took a streetcar to the store, which had opened earlier that week. When I got off the car at Higgins and Main, I saw a line-up in front of our new store. I edged my way up to the front of the line. Upon seeing me, Sam unlocked the door to let me in. The store was jammed with shoppers, and as their purchases were made, they went out through the back door so that the waiting customers could be accommodated.

I was flabbergasted by all the action and sales generated. Sam showed me a full-page advertisement which he had run in the *Winnipeg Free Press* to announce the opening. The result surprised everyone, and showed how starved the populace was for consumer merchandise. In time, the novelty wore off, and sales slowed down to a more moderate pace, but an idea had been born.

Morley came back to Winnipeg from Calgary and joined Sam in the SAAN operation. I continued my efforts in developing General Distributors Ltd. and in hunting down that one, elusive, exclusive agency that would give us volume with a chance for a decent profit. In the past, as new ideas developed, other importers would undercut us in price on a similar product.

Sam was the driving force in expanding the SAAN chain. As the years went by, stores were opened year by year, and by the end of the decade, a total of eight stores were in operation across Manitoba and Saskatchewan. Total sales for the eight stores were $474,636, an average of about $60,000 per store. Although the chain was only marginally profitable, we saw the possibility of building it into one of considerable size. There were, however, many years of trial and error before we struck the winning combination that made SAAN one of the most successful retail chains in Canada.

What SAAN was able to do was to eliminate the middleman and bring big city prices to the smaller towns particularly in Western Canada. It was customary that Sures Brothers, Gaults Limited and quite a number of other well known wholesales would send their salesmen out to the country stores with trunks full of samples. They would sell to the general store keepers on a credit basis and would make a profit of 35%. In turn, the general merchant would mark up the merchandise a further 35% to 40% and finance the farmer until he sold his crops in the fall of the year. This had gone on for generations. It was SAAN who usually worked on one margin of only 35% and who eventually opened stores in most of Western Canada that broke this type of archaic merchandising and brought big city prices to small town Western Canada.

The Acquisition of Metropolitan Stores

The story of our acquiring the large country-wide chain of small variety stores known as Metropolitan was told in great detail in my 1985 book, *The Entrepreneurs*. And since I was forced to close the chain down in the late 1990s, I shall not repeat much of the story. But here are some highlights of what would become a major part of General Distributors for over three decades.

The interest I first expressed in Metropolitan stores in the 1959 brain storming family session, was revived by a story I read in the March, 1960, issue of *Fortune* magazine. The article, entitled "The Looting of the H.L. Green Company," made only minor mention of Metropolitan, the Canadian subsidiary of the H.L. Green Co. of New York, but it was enough to prompt a phone call to Bert Prall, the new chairman of this troubled company.

When Prall came on the line, I introduced myself, explained the purpose of my call, suggested that I was going to be in New York within the week and asked if we could arrange a meeting. In conversation, he mentioned that they had "no intention of selling Metropolitan," as it was one of their best money-making subsidiaries, but as I was going to be in the city, a day and time for an appointment was set up. In the meantime, I talked to brother Harry and asked him if he wished to make the trip, and he agreed to join me.

We were received by Bert Prall in his office. A soft-spoken man in his late fifties or early sixties, Prall's hair was greying, and he was of medium height and fair complexion. After the usual pleasantries, he asked me why I thought they might be interested in selling Metropolitan. I had nothing prepared, but off the cuff, I responded to his question with a leading one of my own:

"When were you last in Canada?"

"I've never been there," he admitted, leaving himself wide open.

"That's a good enough reason. Absentee ownership doesn't often work."

"Okay," he declared. "And what would *you* do with the chain that we are not doing?"

I pulled no punches, saying that of the four well known chains in Canada, Woolworth's, Kresge's, Zellers and Metropolitan, theirs was the most neglected and run down. A whole new image would have to be built with the Canadian consumer. The stores would have to be re-fixtured and renovated. The stores presently operated on a hand-to-mouth basis with minimum stocks, and inventories would have to be jacked up to greater levels.

I also pointed out that the Canadian dollar was being quoted at the time at a 2 or 3 cent premium - an historical fact which must cause pains in any Canadians reading these words in the early 2002. I suggested that they should take their capital out of Canada and put it to work to build up their own operations in the United States.

I mentioned the article in *Fortune* and said, "It's no secret that you have problems at home. Why not put your own house in order, by using the cash you will generate by selling your Canadian subsidiary?" Further- more, Diefenbaker was Prime Minister at the time, and there was much rhetoric about the Americans dominating Canadian business.

Prall listened impassively as I made my case. Then he said he wanted to know more about General Distributors Ltd. I told him that we repre- sented SONY in Canada, and this impressed him. He mentioned that he knew Mr. Ibuka, who was the president of SONY at the time, so we found that we had a common business friend. Evidently, Prall was closely acquainted with The Bank of Tokyo, as was Ibuka, and they had met in Chicago. I gave Ibuka as a reference.

I also asked Prall if he knew Bill Nicks, the chairman of The Bank of Nova Scotia, our bankers. He mentioned that he had met him, so I gave Nicks as a financial reference. We ended our meeting with Prall saying that I had raised some interesting thoughts, and our conversation would be relayed to their board at their next directors' meeting.

One day in November, my secretary told me there was a Mr. Bill Nicks on the line. I wondered why Nicks was calling me. I knew that our loan with the Scotia Bank was in good standing, and thought perhaps it had something to do with information on SONY, since I had been urging him to open an office in Japan. On my last visit to Toronto I had ex- pressed my thoughts that Japan was the emerging giant of Asia, and that many opportunities were going to be available there.

When Nicks came on the phone, I asked him what I could do for him.

"Albert," he said, "I don't know if you can do anything for me, but perhaps I can do something for you. It's about that deal you are working on in New York."

At that moment, I could not understand what he meant.

"I'm working on a couple of deals," I stated. "Which one are you referring to?"

It suddenly dawned on me that the casual meeting with Bert Prall, where I had made some off-the-cuff answers to his questions, had struck a responsive chord and I had given Bill Nicks as my financial reference. Realizing that a deal of this size was usually conducted in a very secretive manner, Nicks probably assumed that I was being coy when I asked him to identify the deal. Immediately, I got my wits about me and decided to probe a bit further.

"What did Bert Prall want to know about me?" I asked.

"He wanted to know if you were good for $20 to $21 million," Nicks declared.

There was a moment's silence, as the enormity of what I had stirred up sank into my consciousness.

"What did you tell him?" I asked. I thought that this was a good opportunity to find out what the Bank of Nova Scotia thought of General Distributors!

"I told Prall that if you had approached him, you probably had a way of putting the deal to bed," said Nicks, tentatively. "You probably have your friend Frawley involved in the deal," he continued. "If you need some financing, the bank will be glad to be of assistance."

I thanked Nicks, and when I hung up, I sat at my desk, stunned for the moment at the size of the venture. From a simple brain storming session, suddenly there was a possibility of consummating a deal, which would be a sensation in the Canadian retail trade. There was only one small problem: ***how do you go about raising $20 million, when your total assets are about half a million?***

I was in a quandary!

The first thing I decided to do was call Bert Prall in New York and find out what prompted his call to Nicks. When I had last seen him, he was quite adamant that they had no intention of selling Metropolitan. When I reached him, I told him of my call from Nicks.

"Albert," he told me, "when I presented to our board of directors your thoughts on Metropolitan, they were quite receptive, and thought it would make sense for H.L. Green. Therefore, would you like to set up a meeting to carry forward our discussion?"

I agreed, and he suggested that the meeting be held in Chicago, in his office in the Federal Reserve Bank Building. This was set for a week later. Wishing to impress him, I told him, "I shall bring my financial team along."

Now the question was, how to go about getting some financial support for this venture? The first thought that occurred to me was to contact Pat Frawley, who, thanks to his sale of Paper-Mate to Gillette, had the required finances to be able to handle a deal of this magnitude. But on reflection, and remembering my past experience with Pat, I closed this avenue of approach and never contacted him.

The second thought was that, perhaps, Howard Webster of Montreal could be the partner for whom I was looking. Webster was independently wealthy and was in a position to handle a deal of this size. But when I contacted him, he declared that retail business was not in one of his preferred investments. At the time he owned the venerable Holt Renfrew chain of stores. Among his other interests he controlled the Schick Eversharp Corporation.

I then thought of Bert Gerstein, the president at the time of Peoples Credit Jewellers, who was in Winnipeg on one of his periodic visits to his store. He was the head of the second largest chain of jewellery stores in Canada, and his father Frank had bought items from us in the late 1940s.

"Albert, it's out of our field," Bert exclaimed, "and the deal is too big for me. Sorry I can't join you, but if you will give me your okay, I would like to contact Sam Fingold, a friend of mine and a great entrepreneur, whom I think would be interested." I told Bert to contact Fingold, and if he was interested, I would arrange to meet with him.

A few days later, I received a call from Fingold. He mentioned that he, too, had been thinking of approaching H.L. Green about their Canadian chain, Metropolitan. He was interested in talking about a joint venture. We arranged to meet at the Hotel Pierre in New York within a couple of days, as he would be there on business. I thought that, if things worked out, we could then proceed to Chicago for the meeting with Prall.

In the meantime, I thought it was time to bring lawyers into the picture, and a financial plan, which I did. But I was concerned to the point that I drafted a letter addressed to Prall, in which I expressed the thought that we would be out of our depth in trying to work out a deal this size. I showed the letter to my brother Sam, who advised not to send it, as something still might turn up.

I soon obtained the interest of James Richardson & Sons, the security underwriters, to possibly finance this acquisition, and I realized now that, with Richardson's interest in the deal, perhaps we *could* handle the financing. Without any formal financial education, and strictly from the great amount of reading that I had been doing, I had a pretty good idea of how these deals were put together.

When our team made our way to Prall's office in the handsome Federal Reserve Bank Building, in the heart of the Chicago financial district, we were suitably impressed. Prall greeted us warmly. I introduced my team, and after my lawyer asked to see the operating statements of the previous five years, I asked Prall what had made the H.L. Green board of directors agree to sell Metropolitan. It seemed that our conversation, and my suggestions at our meeting in New York, had struck a responsive chord when related to Meshulam Riklis of McCrory Corp., who now controlled H.L. Green. Unknown to me, Riklis was looking for financing to buy the Lerner store chain, and this would go a long way towards making the necessary funds available. As a result, Prall was quite adamant that the asking price of $21 million for the Metropolitan chain was reasonable. We left Prall, promising to get in touch with him once we had the chance to study the financial statements he had supplied.

Flying back to Winnipeg on Northwest Airlines and leafing through *Business Week* magazine, I was surprised to read an item reporting that H.L. Green was negotiating for the sale of their Metropolitan stores in Canada. I was flabbergasted, as I felt that secrecy was of the greatest importance at this stage of negotiations. With this news brief, no doubt there would be others in the running to acquire the chain. However, the cat was out of the bag, and there was nothing we could do about it. It became apparent, however, that the sooner we could put the deal together, the better.

What followed was a number of meetings in New York, where our lawyer, Dick Hunter, pointed out to Prall that the price of $21 million was quite out of the question, as it represented considerably more than book value. He intimated to their group that the maximum price that we would be interested in paying was $14.5 million. This represented the fixtures at depreciated cost, inventories, and the properties at depreciated values. I felt that a number of these properties, located in key areas in some of the major cities across Canada, represented excellent value. If the inventory and fixtures could be purchased at depreciated value, then we would not go too far wrong with this price. How we were going to raise this large sum we had not figured out! However, it seemed like an excellent opportunity to become a major factor in the retail chain store business across Canada. This opportunity *could* give us a national presence.

Over the next month, negotiations continued during many meetings in New York. I was the mystery man in the background, the financier, to whom our group had to report, and they used this fact as leverage during negotiations. Finally, a price of $18 million was arrived at. This was related as the final price, non-negotiable.

When this information was brought back to Winnipeg, I said that the price was out of line, and unless it was brought down to a realistic level, I could not see any way that we could make this deal. A realistic deal, in my mind, was $14.5 million. We discovered that H.L. Green owed the Canadian subsidiary $3 million. If we forgave that portion of the debt, what would remain was a $15 million price for the company. Therefore, there was only half a million dollars separating book value from the asking price of the H.L. Green people.

Although we were anxious to keep our negotiations as secret as possible, we soon became aware that Joe Unger, the president of Metropolitan, was also attempting to put together a group to bid for the chain. He was working with Midland Securities of London, Ontario, where the head office of Metropolitan was located.

During these tense and exciting three months of negotiations, I found it necessary to make a trip to Prague, Czechoslovakia, just prior to Christmas, 1960. Irena's father had died, and although she could not risk returning to her native country, I had promised to visit her mother. Enroute, I stopped in Toronto for a number of meetings. When I called Unger to suggest a meeting, at first he said he would not be available.

"*Make* yourself available!" I exclaimed, "After all, you will be reporting to me, as the new controlling interest of Metropolitan."

He got the message and agreed to be in Toronto at the appointed time.

I also arranged a meeting with Cliff Ash of the Bank of Nova Scotia, the purpose of which was to negotiate a loan from the bank for $1 million on behalf of the six brothers, to buy equity in Metropolitan when it was taken public by Richardson's.

In our first meeting, it was obvious that Joe Unger was on guard. As the president of Metropolitan, he was one of a number of prominent businessmen with headquarters in the prosperous, sometimes sleepy city of London, Ontario. Such big companies as Labatt's, Canada Trust and London Life were also headquartered there in those years, and they formed part of an elite society. So *who was this Albert Cohen, who had appeared out of nowhere and was threatening his placid way of life?* The purpose of our meeting was to get acquainted. I assured him that I had no intention of changing management and that he would continue as president of Metropolitan. He asked a number of questions which revealed his general anxiety: one thing that concerned him was whether I intended to use Metropolitan as a vehicle to sell the many import items we were bringing into the country. I assured Unger that his buyers would be the final judge of salability of any items offered. If the values were right and the prices competitive, then they could buy from General Distributors; otherwise, they were free to use their own judgment. Furthermore, as we had the know-how for direct imports, we would impart this knowledge to their buyers, and arrange for them to bring in products from Asia.

My mission was to make peace with Unger, because if successful in the acquisition of Metropolitan, it was necessary for him and his associates to carry on the day-to-day operation, or at least until we could become acquainted with what made the operation tick. After spending a couple of hours with Unger, we parted on good terms - or so I thought. I later found out that he still proceeded to attempt to get a group together to oppose our bid for the acquisition of Metropolitan.

And after all these meetings, I was still in the position where I had to arrange $1 million of personal financing!

The following day I left for Prague. My visit with Irena's mother was dramatic, but without incident. Ever the entrepreneur, and knowing the desire of the communists to establish export connections to earn hard dollars, I arranged the importation of a number of items from Czechoslovakia, which I knew we could sell through General Distributors. I also knew that, if successful in the Metropolitan acquisition, this would be another source of supply that would be welcomed by the Czech authorities, who controlled all exports. While staying at the Alcron Hotel, and knowing that the telephones were being tapped, I arranged for a long distance call to reunite Irena with her mother. They spoke in Czech, and I had the satisfaction of knowing that I had accomplished this reunion. I returned to Winnipeg on December 20, 1960, and promised Irena that I would go back within the year to make progress in bringing her mother to Canada, which was eventually accomplished.

In the meantime, Sam had continued to have discussions with regard to the financing and the offering price to H.L. Green for the Metropolitan acquisition. I was quickly brought up to date, and it was decided, on January 5, 1961, to offer $14.5 million for all the assets of the company. This offer was in letterform, submitted on our behalf by James Richardson & Sons. Accompanying this letter was a fourteen page legal document, prepared by Pitblado, Hoskins, outlining the terms and conditions of the offer.

On this same day, I was asked to sign a letter in which we undertook to purchase not less than 30 per cent of the equity of Metropolitan. In this letter, it stated that Richardson's was acting on our behalf in connection with this acquisition.

Now began the waiting period! The die had been cast, and we were committed if H.L. Green decided to accept this offer. Up to this point in our history, General Distributors had been a family company, known mainly in Manitoba. We had no wealth to speak of; when you take $500,000 in assets and spread it among my parents and the six brothers, it wasn't very much. Today, we give more than that to charity each year. And here, we had gone after a company many times greater than General Distributors. It was a good example of the minnow swallowing the whale.

As the days went slowly by, the question on everyone's mind was, would our offer be accepted?

In the meantime, our lawyer was having one telephone conversation after another with his counterpart in New York. Finally, on the morning of January 23, 1961, Dick Hunter reached me at my office to tell me that it was important that we get together for a meeting, as it looked as if we were going to be outbid on Metropolitan! According to Hunter, he had been informed that unless we raised our bid to $15.5 million, plus the forgiveness of the $3 million owed by the parent company to Metropolitan, making a total of $18.5 million, we would be unsuccessful.

A meeting was hurriedly called and held in the old Trust and Loan building, where the head office of Richardson's was located at the time. Dick related the tone of the telephone conversation and urged in the strongest terms that we should increase our bid by at least $1 million. This was the general consensus of the group. I asked if Sam and I could have a private meeting in an adjoining office.

When we were alone, we evaluated the situation. I felt quite strongly that this was a ploy by the New York group to get us to raise our bid. I could not believe that Unger or anyone else could put together a bid in time. But should we stay with our bid and risk losing the deal, or should we take them at their word and raise our bid? Prall had indicated to Hunter that he felt he owed us the privilege of first refusal, providing we had a competitive bid.

After about ten minutes deliberation, Sam and I agreed that we would raise our bid by $500,000 to $15 million. This was going to be our final bid, and either we would be successful, or we would lose out to some other, unknown group. It was a calculated risk, and I was betting that there was no other serious bidder, but if we were going to make the plunge in acquiring Metropolitan, then it was worth an extra half a million dollars.

When we returned to the meeting and announced our decision, Hunter said, "I think you'll lose the deal."

I replied, "Dick, if we lose the deal, then we lose the deal. Tell New York that this is our final bid; take it or leave it."

We then drafted a telegram to Bert Prall and extended our offer by one day to January 24th, 1961. We decided to put them on the spot, to either accept or reject our offer. The next day, we called the other brothers at their various offices and advised them of the latest turn of events.

On January 24th, another period of waiting began. The hours passed slowly. Soon it was 3:00 p.m. in Winnipeg, still no call, and we were chewing our nails. When by 4:00 p.m. there still had been no call, Sam and I discussed the fact that it was 5:00 p.m. in New York, and that would be the close of business.

"I just can't believe that we've lost the deal!" I told Sam. "This seems to have been *meant* for us. I just can't understand it. Could we have been overbid?"

Sam saw how deeply disappointed I was and tried to cheer me up by saying, "You know, Albert, maybe it's for the best. It's a big deal, and maybe we could have gotten into trouble. Don't worry, other deals will come about."

As we spoke, the hour was slipping by. Suddenly, we both jumped as the phone rang. I picked up the receiver and heard the excited voice of Norman Alexander, the General Manager of James Richardson, who were acting on our behalf, on the other end of the line:

"Congratulations, Albert. You've just acquired a chain of retail stores."

It seems that Prall and his team had waited to the last moment, choosing the closing time of 5:00 p.m. in Winnipeg, which was 6:00 p.m. in New York.

Sam and I shook hands and then looked at each other. The commitment was confirmed, and the work was just beginning. Now the next phase had to be accomplished: our personal financing had to be arranged. Although I had requested a loan from the Bank of Nova Scotia of $1 million, I still had not received a reply. Also, not to disturb the present management of Metropolitan, it was necessary that they be made aware that we would work closely with them. Lawyers, transfer agents, trust companies, banks and countless other matters had to be attended to.

The doubts began to creep into our thinking. Had we bitten off more than we could chew? We were risking everything we had built up over the years, and were going into debt for $1 million. Yet I had a gut feeling that the decision was right.

It was still important to keep the deal secret, but this seemed to be impossible, as the rumours soon started to circulate. Because of the size of the deal, I thought it best that, for the meantime, the press release should be to the effect that Richardson's had bought the chain. They agreed, and consequently the stories broke across Canada on March 3, 1961, that James Richardson & Sons had acquired Metropolitan for the sum of $18 million. No mention was made in the press release that it was on our behalf. No doubt we caused some embarrassment to Richardson's, as, of course, they had no intention of going into the retail business!

After considering a number of different methods of financing, a plan was approved by all concerned. The great leverage we had was that the real estate was all mortgage-free.

Gendis was now to be the controlling interest of *eighty-seven variety stores* with a long history. This, I gleaned from the prospectus issued by James Richardson & Sons, from which I quote a few fascinating facts:

> The Metropolitan organization had its origin in 1908 when F.H. Brewster opened his first store in St. Thomas, Ontario. Other stores were opened subsequently under the name F.H. Brewster Company in London, Ingersoll, Chatham and other Ontario cities, and in 1915 the chain was sold to a company known as The Canadian Smallwares Limited.
>
> During 1920, Metropolitan 5 cent to 50 cent Stores Incorporated of the United States purchased control of Canadian Smallwares Limited and merged that company with The Variety 5 cent to 10 cent Store of Montreal to form Metropolitan Stores Limited, a company incorporated under the laws of Canada on May 11, 1920. At the time of incorporation, the Metropolitan organization operated a total of eleven stores in southwestern Ontario and the Province of Quebec.

In 1930, Metropolitan 5 cent to 50 cent Stores Incorporated sold its Canadian subsidiary to F.W. Grand Silver Stores Inc. of the United States, and this latter company was purchased in 1933 by the H.L. Green Company, also of the United States. Shortly thereafter, the name Metropolitan disappeared in the United States, but in Canada the name Metropolitan Stores had remained since 1920.

During the period of almost forty-one years of United States ownership, the Metropolitan organization has shown substantial growth. The company now operates eighty-seven variety stores in all provinces of Canada, with the exception of Newfoundland. The company is one of the four largest variety chain organizations in Canada, directing its operations from executive offices located in London, Ontario.

This brief synopsis of Metropolitan was illuminating. First of all, with General Distributors assuming control of Metropolitan, not only were we bringing back to Canada a company from the United States, but we had suddenly become a major player in the retailing business in this country.

As the word leaked out of the financing, there was a ground swell of demand for the equity soon to be issued. Richardson's indicated that the common stock would be priced at $6.00 per share. A market developed on over the counter trading on an "as when issued" basis in the $8.00 to $8.50 range.

It was April, 1961, when Bert Prall and his group arrived in Winnipeg to participate in the closing of our deal, for which accommodation was arranged at the Fort Garry Hotel. The signing went smoothly, and four cheques totaling $13,638,189.63 were turned over to Prall. This was the total after taking into consideration $3,596,236 of the net assets excluded from the agreement of sale.

When the securities were brought to market, the issue was an instant success. The $6.5 million issue of mortgage bonds was placed primarily with insurance companies. The common stock immediately rose from the issue price of $6 per share to $8.00.

Without the team that had been put together, all talented Winnipegers, the repatriation of Metropolitan to Canada would not have been possible. Everyone eventually gained from their involvement. It was the first financing to have been done for a merchandise company by

Richardson's, who in the past had specialized primarily in bringing to market mining and oil stocks. Their help and cooperation was invaluable. This was the beginning of a long and mutually beneficial relationship although we would have our tensions, even a nasty court case, in later years.

From what had been an impossible dream, we now controlled one of the leading retailers in Canada, listed on both the Toronto and Montreal stock exchanges. From a family business, responsible to only ourselves, now we had many shareholders to whom we were responsible and who had placed their confidence in the abilities of the six Cohen brothers. **We knew we could not let down their trust in us!**

When I became chairman of the board, Joe Unger carried on as president of the new company. His attitude was a wary one, as he did not know what to expect in the way of policy from the new control. Were we raiders out for the fast buck, as so many acquisitors had been in the past, or did we mean what we said, when we assured him that it was our intention to build Metropolitan into one of the top merchandising organizations in Canada? Only time would tell.

In discussions with brother Sam, who had a natural talent for architectural design, we decided to use Winnipeg as a pilot store and bring it into what we referred to as The *New Met* Image. New types of lighting, merchandise displays and sales methods were tested, and also new lines of merchandise were introduced. The old type of restaurant was replaced with a modern lunch counter, where the meals were prepared on new, modern equipment which was visible to the customers being served. New signs outdoors and inside were made. The sales increase was almost immediate. This renovation program was innovated in many of the company owned stores. Jim Suzuki and his construction crew, under the guidance of Maurice Angelle, traveled across Canada for two years, making many of the old Met stores blossom forth under The *New Met* Image.

Many SAAN store executives were drafted into service during this drive to establish the changes in Metropolitan. It soon became evident that the SAAN personnel, who were devoting much of their time and energy, should become part of the new Metropolitan group.

Discussions began to take place with regard to a merger with SAAN, which was at that time a chain of twenty-two stores privately owned by the Cohen brothers. This was brought up at the first Metropolitan annual meeting, which was held on April 25, 1962, at the Marlborough Hotel in Winnipeg.

The reaction from Joe Unger was lukewarm, as it seemed to confirm that we were anxious to sell off one of our privately held companies to Met. This was contrary to what we knew was the case, since after one year of ownership, we realized that turning Metropolitan around was a major job. Sam and his associates at SAAN were devoting more and more of their time without charging any of this to Met.

We approached Richardson's to put a value on the SAAN acquisition. I called Jim Richardson and told him that I wanted to deal strictly at arm's length. Jim, in turn, had the acquisition valued by Morgan Guaranty in New York, strictly on a financial statement basis. The valuation they submitted showed a range of 119,921 shares on the low side, to 145,000 on the high side, if the deal was to be consummated on the basis of a share exchange.

I spoke to the brothers and persuaded them that this merger would be to the benefit of all concerned, and on August 31, 1962, at a special shareholders meeting, the merger was confirmed. As we wished to be beyond reproach, we agreed to take the smallest amount of stock recommended. By acquiring this additional stock, we now owned about 48 per cent of the common stock of Met, and I felt we were in a much safer position as far as control was concerned.

At the second annual meeting, held in April, 1963, brother Sam was named to the board of directors and appointed executive vice-president. A very important decision was made to move the head office from London, Ontario, to Montreal. Why? Since Montreal, not London, was the prime source of soft good manufacturers and import suppliers, it was felt that it would be very much to the advantage of the company to be located there. We moved the people who wanted to move, and those who didn't were paid off. Morley was asked to try and locate suitable acreage, and ten acres were acquired fronting the Trans Canada Highway. Sam, working with Cecil Blankstein and David Thordarson, designed an office-warehouse building, which was to become the design that was used in the major cities across Canada for SONY and our head office in Winnipeg.

The company prospered, but dividends were not paid, as all cash flow from depreciation and earnings was plowed back to further the growth of the company. The shareholders were rewarded by the excellent appreciation of the stock. A brief example will suffice: someone who purchased 1,000 shares of Metropolitan at $6 a share and stayed with it, saw it split three for one and eventually reach $26 per share. So the original $6,000 investment ended up being worth $78,000.

Under the able leadership of brothers Sam and Morley - both would serve as presidents of the firm. Metropolitan continued to prosper through the 1960s. Through experimentation, a plan began to evolve as to the type of merchandise that should be carried in the larger Metropolitan stores and the smaller SAAN units. In trying to emulate K-Mart and the Woolco Stores, who were building larger units, we found that Met could not merchandise stores properly that were larger than 40,000 square feet. White goods, such as fridges, washing machines, dryers, furniture and garden tools, which were carried by K-Mart and Woolco, did not fit into our type of merchandising niche. The Met prospered, being the dominant store in smaller communities, where the population was too small to support the large discount stores.

At the same time, SAAN was evolving an image of its own. There was a general upgrading of merchandise, together with new types of fixtures and shelving, and clearer labeling and signage. The chain was growing rapidly and was being recognized by shoppers as an outlet that offered good values at reasonable prices, whereas the department stores were cutting back on services to try and save on expenses to meet the intense competition from the new discounters. SAAN was offering free parking and service by pleasant clerks in easily accessible shopping malls. SAAN could be profitable on mark-ups of at least 20 per cent less than the department stores, and as we began to cluster stores in order to reduce the cost of advertising, sales and profits continued to grow. The department stores, in having to achieve higher grosses and at the same time reduce services, were caught in a "Catch 22" situation. The recent deaths of K-Mart and even Eaton's prove the point I was making.

General Distributors Acquires the Greenberg Chain

In the meantime, while looking for a possible acquisition, Morley brought to my attention the rumour that the Greenberg chain of stores, headquartered in Montreal, might be available. The company was listed on the Montreal Stock Exchange, having gone public in August, 1965, at $4.50 per share.

In my experience, I knew that it was much more difficult to acquire a family-owned business than a company such as Metropolitan, where one was dealing with a financial organization. I realized that, in approaching Michael Greenberg, I would be dealing with the founder of a company who had devoted his lifetime to building his chain of stores. I was aware that I had to tread lightly in dealing with Greenberg's ego, regardless of how good the offer might be.

In researching the early history of Greenberg's, I learned that in 1918, Michael Greenberg, at the tender age of twenty, opened a small dry goods store in the St. Henri neighborhood of Montreal. As additional stores were opened and the chain expanded, he brought in his two younger brothers, Louis and Albert. Louis, the youngest, did not get along too well with Michael, and when Albert, the middle brother, died, the partnership with Louis was dissolved. Michael retained Greenberg Stores Ltd., while Louis formed the A.L. Green Stores, which competed in many of the same towns where Greenberg stores were located. I determined that, if I had a positive reaction after meeting with Michael and his son, Buddy, I would then have James Richardson & Sons, together with our auditors, develop a pro forma statement to show what price we could offer for the Greenberg acquisition.

When Morley and I first called on Michael Greenberg at the head office location, 9150 Park Avenue, we were ushered into his rather overlarge office. He rose to greet me: a man close to seventy, short, balding and rotund. He had a light grey moustache, wore spectacles, and welcomed me with a warm but reserved smile. His son Melvin, or Buddy as he was known, occupied the smaller, adjoining office. Morley, the "Montreal brother," knew both of the Greenbergs on a social basis.

After we passed the time of day to get acquainted, Buddy joined us, and I then broached the subject of the merging of Greenberg into Metropolitan. When I suggested that there could be cash, as well as General Distributors stock involved, the Greenberg reaction was that if a deal were to be made, it would have to be all cash. They were aware that Metropolitan, which had first gone public in 1962, had increased from the initial issue price of $6 per share to $18.

I of course, preferred an all cash deal, because that would mean that there would be no dilution of common stock. Because General Distributors Ltd. at this time controlled only 48 percent of Metropolitan's common shares, it was in our interest to buy on a cash basis. If we borrowed the money for the purchase, this could always be repaid. Once stock was issued, it could be bought back only by purchasing it on the open market.

It became evident that Michael, like any founder of a company, was of two minds. There was the temptation to sell his stock far above the market price. However, there was the pride of retaining control of his company and seeing it grow under the leadership of his only son, Buddy. Michael ran his company in a very autocratic manner. He supervised all the buying, and no commitment in ordering merchandise could be made without his consent. He was involved in every facet of the business, from buying to advertising to store supervision. He would drop in unexpected to any of the twenty Greenberg stores, and every manager knew that the store he was responsible for had *better* be in good shape, or he would feel the wrath of Michael. His was truly a one-man operation. His son was dominated by his father, and usually trailed along in his footsteps. Like so many domineering, self-made men, Michael found it difficult to let go of the reins. It was only because Buddy wanted someone he could turn to for advice and leadership, once his father was not there to guide him, that any consideration was being given to a possible sale of Greenberg's.

Sensing all this, and feeling that it was important for Metropolitan to expand into this market, I was determined to try my best to humour Michael Greenberg and attempt to consummate a deal. When I asked if I could see their confidential statements for the past five years, he was not very forthcoming and advised me that all that would be made available was their audited statement for their public shareholders. I then asked if I could send my financial team to meet with his controller and see if we could put together an offer for their controlling shares. He acceded to that request, and that ended our formal meeting.

When Edson Boyd, who spearheaded the financial group, returned from his meeting with the Greenbergs, he told me that he had a better reception than he had anticipated. He received quite a bit of information, which made it possible for us to put together a formal offer for the Greenberg chain.

At a subsequent meeting arranged in Montreal, I presented an offer of $7.00 per share for their controlling interest. This was for the 65 per cent of the stock controlled by the Greenbergs, or 400,000 shares, a total of $2.8 million. The balance of 35 per cent of the shares was owned by various funds and smaller shareholders, which had been sold through Maison Placements. Michael said that the company was worth more, and that he would not be interested in selling at that price. I then asked him what he thought the company was worth, but he refused to name a price. I finally indicated to Michael that we would raise our price to $7.50 per share, take it or leave it. This was 50 cents per share more than we had figured the company was worth in the figures we had put together.

"Not enough," was Michael Greenberg's reply.

Finally, in exasperation, I asked him to name a final price, and I would indicate if we had any further room to negotiate.

Michael declared, "If you want to conclude a deal, I'll take $8.00 per share." He had finally named his price, and now it was up to me to decide if I should accept his offer, or take it back to Winnipeg for consideration. I realized that if I did not make a fast decision, he could well change his mind.

I therefore extended my hand and said, "Michael, you have just made a deal. I accept your offer at $8.00 per share. It is now important that we keep everything very confidential, so that word does not leak out to the public, as we do not want the stock to run away on us."

We agreed that, until a formal offer was put together and presented to the Greenbergs, no discussion would take place with anyone except our lawyers. A date was set for a formal meeting to be held in Montreal, in the offices of Phillips, Vineberg & Co., who were the legal counsel for the Greenbergs. This law firm also acted for Metropolitan, and besides being a director on the board of Greenberg Stores Ltd., Philip Vineberg was a personal friend of brother Morley. Vineberg was wearing two hats in this transaction, although officially he was acting on behalf of Greenberg's interests.

When I returned to Winnipeg and reported the results of my meeting, it now became necessary to arrange the financing for this deal. Taking into consideration that we would follow up with an offer to buy out the minority shareholders at the same price per share, the total purchase price would be in the neighborhood of $5 million. As the Canadian Imperial Bank of Commerce were the main bankers to Metropolitan, and the Greenberg deal would be an acquisition by Metropolitan, it was decided we would give this bank the first opportunity to do the interim financing of $5 million.

Whereas, six years earlier, the financing of the Metropolitan acquisition by General Distributors had presented a major problem, it was very heartening to see that, in a matter of a few days, I received confirmation that the money was available to make the Greenberg acquisition at any time we wished to call for it. Our growing company now had credibility, and because Metropolitan was a publicly listed company on the Montreal and Toronto stock exchanges, and had performed well over the years since its public offering, the doors had been opened for financing that was not available to us before as a private company.

It now became a matter of waiting for the report of our investigation teams, who were touring and inspecting the various Greenberg stores. Finally, the report came, and Morley related to me that everything seemed to be in order, and, in his opinion, we should proceed with the deal.

Now a final meeting with the Greenbergs was necessary to arrange a closing date, finalize matters and conclude our deal. Rumours seemed to be circulating, as they always seem to do when something is in the wind. The price of Greenberg stock started to climb on the Montreal Stock Exchange and was now selling at $6.50 per share. Obviously, if the stock rose to the $7.00 or $8.00 level, I could visualize the Greenbergs wishing to back away from their verbal commitment, and demand a higher price for their stock. Time was of the essence to finalize the deal. I therefore asked for a meeting to be arranged at the offices of Phillips, Vineberg & Co. to nail it down.

When I arrived in Montreal late in the afternoon of July 26, 1967, Morley met me at the airport. After checking in to the hotel, he invited me to have dinner at the Elm Ridge Golf Club. It was there that I happened to see Philip Vineberg, who had just come off the golf course. Over a drink, I mentioned the meeting we had scheduled the next morning in his office.

"Albert," he said sadly. "I hate to tell you this, but I think you are here on a wild goose chase."

"Why?" I asked him, surprised by his remark.

"Simply because I don't think that my client wants to make a deal. I saw him last night, and he was very upset."

"I'll see you tomorrow, and we'll see how things work out," I said, as I left him. This was certainly an unexpected turn of events, and I realized that I would have to be extremely cautious in negotiations the next day.

On July 27, 1967, we met in the boardroom of Phillips, Vineberg, which was located in the Royal Bank Building, 1 Place Ville Marie. Present were brothers Morley and Sam, Edson Boyd, Dick Hunter, Michael Greenberg, Buddy Greenberg, Phil Vineberg and myself. I opened the conversation by stating that we were assembled to conclude the purchase by Metropolitan of the common shares of Greenberg Stores Ltd. I had given up the talk of a merger, in view of the fact that we were arranging a cash purchase. It was very evident that the Greenbergs were quite unsophisticated when it came to dealing in financial matters. Michael Greenberg then declared that he wanted a few questions answered before we went on. I asked what they were.

"How about a five-year contract for Buddy and thirty months for me?" Without hesitation, I answered, "You've got it."

"I've made certain charitable contributions through Greenberg's, which have not been paid yet," he went on. "Will you honour them?"   "Of course we will," I replied.

"I have a chauffeur and a company Lincoln car. Will I be permitted to keep them, if the sale is concluded?"

I realized that these were inconsequential matters, and I was not going to give Greenberg a chance to back out of his commitment, so I readily agreed to this request.

"You are agreeing to everything that I'm asking for," Michael went on, "so if Buddy agrees, I guess we have a deal." Buddy nodded his head affirmatively, and we then shook hands around the table.

I then asked Hunter to phone the Canadian Imperial Bank of Commerce, who were standing by, ready to send their manager over with a certified cheque for $3.2 million. This sum was based on the 400,000 shares the Greenberg family controlled, at $8.00 per share.

When the manager quickly brought over the cheque, I glanced at it and then handed it over to Michael Greenberg. He took the cheque, and without even looking at it, folded it and threw it over to Buddy, saying, "Here. It's your cheque, not mine."

It was a gesture which seemed to be painfully suggesting, "My lifetime of work is represented in this piece of paper." There was a moment of silence after this action. We then proceeded with the necessary signing of the various agreements.

To finance this acquisition, Newt Hughes of Richardson Securities was of the opinion that we could market $3 million in a new preferred issue of stock. This would be known as 1967 Metropolitan Preferred, to pay a dividend of $1.30 per share. The issue would consist of 150,000 shares at $20.00 per share. The balance of $1.8 million for the minority shares to be acquired would be bank financed out of our regular line of credit. These 1967 preferred shares were marketed successfully. This was probably the last issue of a straight preferred to be sold to the public. Years later, any preferred share issue had to have some convertible feature to be marketed successfully.

The Wonderful Growth of SAAN Stores

SAAN Stores Ltd. showed excellent growth, both in sales and profitability, in the decade of the seventies. By 1970, SAAN was operating fifty-four stores and generating sales of $10,868,000, an average of $201,000 per store. By the end of the decade, the SAAN chain had grown to 113 stores, with sales of $52,361,000, an average of $463,337,000 per store, up 130 per cent.

As the rapid growth of SAAN stores continued, we found that we had outgrown our head office at 791 Notre Dame Avenue. Often, in order to service the stores, merchandise being readied had to be processed on the driveway. It was about this time that it became apparent that we would either have to rent or build a new facility to house the expansion of SAAN. At the same time, SONY sales were growing quickly, and we were in an upward growth cycle year by year.

It was decided to secure acreage sufficient to take care of our future needs. After considering a number of locations, a final decision was made to acquire six acres of land opposite the new McLeod's headquarters, located off McGillvray Boulevard in the Fort Garry area. Additional land was negotiated from the town of Fort Garry by Sam, to a total of twenty acres. Sam then proceeded to work with our architects, Green, Blankstein, Russell and Associates, to plan our new head office at 1370 SONY Place. Work was started in the early months of 1969 to have the new head office ready in time for the 1970s.

In 1970, an additional five SAAN stores were opened, now raising the total to fifty-four, and by the end of 1976 there were seventy-three stores in the chain.

My brother Sam had become very involved in civic affairs and was responsible for acting as chairman of the St. Boniface Hospital Research Institute. There was no question of the worthiness of the cause, but as it was occupying most of his time, I made the remark that if he would spend this time in furthering the growth of SAAN, the results would soon become apparent.

I did not dream how seriously Sam would take this comment. Suddenly, he turned his merchandising talent to furthering the growth of the SAAN chain. He noted that SAAN had already outgrown its alloted space in the warehouse for the processing of merchandise and requested approval for an extension of 70,000 square feet to be added to our recently constructed building. It was completed and occupied by 1977.

In the ensuing years, the growth of SAAN was sensational. Sam had developed a distinct signage and colouring scheme for the interior of the stores and issued an edict that the stores should be well stocked at all times. The SAAN chain was soon well known in all four western provinces and later made an impact in northwestern Ontario.

It is obvious that SAAN's success is due to the fact that it meets the needs of the shopping public. The stores range in size from 7,000 to 10,000 square feet. Usually well located in high-traffic centres, they are easily identifiable by their signage - the name SAAN is repeated either in red or in sequence as a red and green border across the face and entrance of the stores. The stores are well stocked with popular-styled merchandise, catering to the middle class customer, and merchandising ladies', men's and children's wear. SAAN works on a standard mark-up, on a policy of one price regardless of where a store is located, and the values are soon apparent to the price conscious shopper. The person shopping at a SAAN store in Prince George, B.C. can buy the same item at the same price as in all of the many Winnipeg stores.

Whereas department stores require a far higher mark-up on their merchandise, to pay for their higher cost of operation, SAAN can work on a much lower margin. SAAN offers personal clerical help in shopping, a service that was missing not only in the department stores, but also in the mammoth Woolco, K-Mart and Zeller stores.

As I like to put it, "rather than have the customer come to the stores, the SAAN stores, because of their handy locations, come to the customer."

There is no question that Sam was the driving force in the growth of SAAN. It was under his direction that the processing warehouse was built. His relentless energy in supervising every facet of this organization, and his insistence on perfection, was well known by all employees. The SAAN success is a measure of Sam's energy and ambition in creating a successful organization.

I must emphasize that some of the other brothers' involvement in the early, formative years of SAAN was most important. It was Harry's partnership with Ralph Kalef in the first War Surplus Store in Calgary that gave the inspiration for the opening of the first SAAN store in 1947.

In Vancouver, Joe was involved in obtaining new store locations since the early days of the founding of SAAN, many of them former Safeway locations of under 10,000 square feet. Over the years, Chauncey in Toronto often managed to obtain good sources of supply for the stores.

Before he moved to Montreal in 1954, Morley worked very closely with Sam in the years he was associated with SAAN. It was this retail experience that stood him in good stead, so that when Metropolitan was acquired in 1962, he could take a managing role in this important acquisition. Thanks to Morley, we were able to bring the Met stores from the thirties into modern-day merchandising. He had a good sense of what the public wants, as shown by the fact that the Met chain grew from $20 million volume in 1962 to over $130 million in the mid-1980s. It took many years and millions of dollars in experimentation to decide what type of store Met should be. Originally, they were predominantly in downtown areas, but we eventually realized that downtown stores were a dying breed. Instead, we found our niche: 25,000 to 35,000 square foot stores in *smaller* communities, where we rapidly became the leading junior department store.

All in all, SAAN had been a very successful venture, with input from all the brothers, but unquestionably this has been Sam's baby. Over the years it has matured to a full grown member of the Gendis family of companies.

After the signing of the joint venture with SONY, we could consolidate only 51 per cent of sales and earnings. I therefore reasoned that this would be a good opportunity to make an offer for the minority shares of Metropolitan. If we were successful in our bid, then we would be able to consolidate 100 per cent of sales and earnings instead of the 63 per cent, which we now owned, having bought stock on the open market from time to time.

By July 4, 1977, General Distributors owned 100 per cent of the common shares of Metropolitan Stores of Canada Ltd.

From the year 1978, all Metropolitan sales, which of course included its wholly-owned subsidiaries, SAAN and Greenberg's, were consolidated 100 per cent in General Distributors. The ensuing years proved the wisdom of this move. Sales grew rapidly in the retail store division. The consolidation gave General Distributors much greater maneuverability.

Not that we didn't make a few major errors. One of our acquisitions during the 1970s was the A.L. Green Ltd. chain, the offshoot of the separation of the original Greenberg Stores Ltd. When I was approached to consider this acquisition, A.L. Green was in financial difficulties. I felt, however, that only if it could be merged into Metropolitan and Greenberg's, would it be worthy of consideration. A.L. Green was the chain of stores that had been developed by Michael Greenberg's brother Louis, when their partnership had been dissolved. It was in 1972 that Morley had arranged an appointment for me to meet Louis Greenberg, with the intention of discussing the possible acquisition of his chain and its addition to the Greenberg group. In many towns, the stores competed head to head, and it was felt that if the chain was acquired, in some cases, one store could serve the community instead of two.

After some deliberation, it was decided that we would offer to buy control and offer $1.75 a share. For approximately $2.5 million, we now owned and controlled the A.L. Green chain. Now it became necessary to examine and analyze carefully what we had bought in this acquisition, and it soon became evident that we had acquired more than we had bargained for. We found that inventories had been overstated, and that there were a few disputes about leases, where negotiations would have to be entered into with the landlords, in order to clear up items in question.

All our acquisitions had been successful up to this time, and we had become complacent in thinking that we were infallible and could turn around any situation. The further we checked into the A.L. Green acquisition, the more we realized that we had bagged "a can of worms." But there was nothing we could do. It now was ours, and we had to make the best of the situation.

As in all things, there were pluses as well as minuses in the A.L. Green acquisition. We realized that much more caution would have to be used in any future acquisitions, since from a financial point of view, we had overpaid for the assets of A.L. Green. More and deeper investigation would have revealed how sick this corporation was. But we learned a lesson that would prevent us from making a more serious mistake in future acquisitions. There were further silver linings: an exceptional low cost-fixed lease on the A.L. Green warehouse, which led to the Greenberg warehouse being closed and merged into the A.L. Green facility, thereby effecting substantial savings. Furthermore, a number of A.L. Green store leases were written when rents were reasonable. Both Greenberg's and Metropolitan eventually benefited from these stores, which became part of their operation.

General Distributors of Canada Ltd. Goes Public

After the acquisition of the Greenberg chain by Metropolitan, our retail group consisted of eighty two Metropolitan stores, fifty four SAAN stores and twenty four Greenberg stores, for a total of 160 retail outlets. Sales generated by the group totaled $64,659,238 as of the year-end 1969. Earnings after tax were $2,018,369. Because we controlled 48 per cent of Metropolitan, we could only consolidate 48 per cent of the earnings of the retail chain in General Distributors. Earnings per common share after payment of the preferred dividend were $1.94 per share. These figures compare most favourably with the following statistics compiled when Metropolitan was first acquired in 1961: sales at that time were $20,492,362, profits were $204,132 and earnings per share 28 cents. No dividends were paid on the common shares, as all cash flow was put back to further the growth of the company.

It was in 1963 that a new federal registered company was formed and named General Distributors of Canada Ltd. to act as the holding company for the various subsidiaries. General Distributors Ltd. still operated as an Alberta provincially incorporated company involved in the import business. This company was 100 per cent owned by General Distributors of Canada Ltd., which also owned 48 per cent of the common stock of Metropolitan Stores of Canada Ltd.

It was in 1967, after the acquisition of Greenberg's, that I began to think seriously of taking General Distributors of Canada Ltd. public. The company was continuing to grow at a rapid pace, and there was a need for additional financing. Furthermore, although the brothers' reputations were growing as men of means, all their resources were tied up in the company. We all went into personal debt to acquire Metropolitan. The only way to get any funds into our own hands was by marketing some of the equity we owned.

In 1968, we approached Newt Hughes on the question of Richardson's taking General Distributors public. All the financial statements were supplied for their analysis. After evaluating the information, Newt informed me that the following steps would have to be taken in order for Richardson's to make a successful offering: first, the equity owned by General Distributors in Metropolitan would have to be increased from 48 to over 50 per cent. Second, as the SONY contract only had four years to go before expiring, it would be necessary to obtain a new ten year contract from SONY Corporation, Tokyo. If these two requirements were met, then Hughes felt certain that Richardson's would be glad to act as underwriters to take General Distributors public, at a price to be determined at a later date.

I immediately began to purchase Met common shares. Shares that we had sold in our original marketing at $6 each now cost us $18 and $24 a share, in order to bring our equity position up to 50.3 per cent of the outstanding common stock. This would allow us to consolidate sales and earnings of Metropolitan with General Distributors.

The great hurdle remaining was to approach Akio Morita to ask him to cancel a contract that still had four years to go, and replace it with a new, ten year contract. I had every confidence that Morita would accede to my request when I explained the reason and the importance of being able to take our company public.

A meeting was arranged in Tokyo. Morita listened to my explanation and shook his head with a smile.

"Albert," he said, "your contract still has almost half of the time before expiration. My board of directors may object to this unusual request."

"Akio," I replied, "I know they will listen to you. Please explain the importance of my request. By going public, for the first time we will have some financial independence. I'll consider it a great personal favour. Without a new ten year contract, our company cannot be taken public."

Morita said he would let me know before I returned to Canada. Fortunately, Ed Rosiny was visiting in Tokyo at the time, and before my departure he called to say that Morita had instructed him to draw up a new ten year contract for General Distributors. Again, Morita let me set the terms, and I returned to Winnipeg with the new contract. This removed any obstacle to the marketing of the company; the contract was dated February 21, 1968, to run to March 31, 1978. Gendis was designated as the exclusive distributor in Canada for transistor radios, tape recorders, television sets, packaged stereo units and hi-fi receivers and components.

On May 10, 1968, Richardson Securities of Canada offered 435,000 shares of General Distributors to the public at $7 per share. The offering was an immediate success, with the stock almost doubling in value within the space of a few months. The success of the Metropolitan common share offering had clearly established our reputation, and we now had a good following in the investment world. Indeed, if someone had purchased 1,000 shares for $7,000, he or she would see it split two for one, and then four for three, making it 2,666 shares. There was a further split of two for one that made the original issue of 1,000 shares to be 5,332 shares. As Gendis shares reached a high of $27.00, the original shares rose to a value of $143,964!

By the end of the decade, sales of General Distributors of Canada Ltd. and subsidiary companies totaled $83,092,048, and net earnings were $1,914,491, which equated to 61 cents per share. Sales and earnings were consolidated with the 50 per cent ownership of Metropolitan. Once that 50 per cent control had been secured, not only did we make available to Metropolitan the resources and know how of SAAN stores buyers, but I also felt that we should encourage direct imports from Asia of many items that they were buying from middlemen located in Toronto and Montreal. The Tokyo office, under the management of Frank Wertheimber, could be used to source many of the hard goods and toys that Met was selling, and which represented a good portion of its volume.

Consequently, I arranged for Met executive Bob Hallam to accompany me on one of my periodic trips to Japan. We visited many of the factories and suppliers, and soon a good portion of our products was being imported directly. This tended not only to increase volume, but also profitability. Roland Giroux, a vice-president in charge of merchandising for Metropolitan, also made a number of trips to Asia. As the years progressed, Wertheimber accompanied the Metropolitan buyers to Taiwan, Hong Kong and South Korea to expand our contacts there.

In summary, the decade of the sixties was a most important growth period for company enterprises. The groundwork was laid for the future growth of the seventies and eighties decades which would propel General Distributors of Canada Ltd. to one of the top 200 companies in Canada. We now had two companies listed on the Toronto and Montreal stock exchanges.

In this decade, not only had we seen and participated in the phenomenal growth of SONY, but we had acquired two major chains: Metropolitan and Greenberg's. SAAN had begun to establish itself as a force in the soft goods marketplace. Plans were underway to build new office warehouses for SONY in Toronto, Montreal and Vancouver, as well as the new head office in Winnipeg. All in all, the 1960s had proven to be a most eventful, profitable decade.

On the personal level, it was an eventful decade as well. In the summer of 1960, the entire family had met in Calgary to celebrate the fiftieth wedding anniversary of our parents, a gala event, with all the brothers, wives and grandchildren present.

Later, in the same decade, our second son, James Eduard, was born on June 3, 1966, followed by our third child, Anna-Lisa, on December 5, 1967. Anthony had been born on May 29, 1958.

Our extended family was diminished, however, with the loss of our beloved mother, who had ailed for two years before passing away in September, 1968, in Calgary, with father and all six sons at her bedside. She had reached the age of seventy-eight. She was the matriarch of the family, and her belief in the ultimate success of her six sons working together as a unit was justified. Together with my father, it was their vision and driving personalities which was the binding force responsible for the survival of General Distributors in those early, formative years. We were all grateful that mother lived long enough to enjoy some of the success she inspired.

My father passed away June 2, 1973. He attended the opening of our headquarters in Winnipeg then known as the SONY Building at 1370 SONY Place. The ribbon cutting ceremony was the ceremony which gave him so much pleasure. It was Akio Morita together with Premier Schreyer who did the honour. They were gracious in complementing father for his part in the early success of the company.

Today, the building is known as the Gendis Building but bears the same address of 1370 SONY Place in recognition of its early headquarters of SONY of Canada Ltd.

The Demise of Metropolitan and Greenberg Stores

One of the most difficult decisions that I had to make in my business career was to put Greenberg Stores who controlled Metropolitan Stores into receivership. This was a decision that our Board of Directors decided in January 1997. The retail chain was bleeding the parent company Gendis Inc.

Once the board made the decision final, I took charge and decided that we would protect our good name and make sure that the only one that would be hurt would be Gendis Inc. It was Gendis Inc. who acted as the banker to all our subsidiaries. In its day, we did all the financing for the SONY growth in Canada. This included the SONY Stores that we founded which grew to a very successful retail chain featuring all SONY products.

The simple reason was that Gendis, as the parent company, charged the prime bank rate plus 1/2% to each of its subsidiaries. This was a source of revenue for Gendis as Gendis borrowed its money on the street. The Gendis notes were evaluated by and received a worthy credit rating by the Dominion Bond Rating Service. Our notes in turn, were backed by the five major Canadian banks. These were the Bank of Nova Scotia, the Canadian Imperial Bank of Commerce, the Bank of Montreal, the Royal Bank of Canada and the Toronto Dominion Bank.

The *roots* of the collapse of some of our proudest achievements, the purchases and building-up of many Metropolitan and Greenberg Stores, lay in the not-so-distant past. It was in 1992, when Prime Minister Brian Mulroney had introduced the Goods and Services Tax (GST), which took the then-hidden sales tax and made it suddenly visible. All retail sales, with a few exceptions, were subject to this tax, on top of which was placed the provincial sales tax (PST), which varied in rates from province to province. Alberta, as always, was an exception to this, because of her energy wealth, they did not have a sales tax—but they were still subject to the now very visible GST.

Interestingly, the GST was a fairer tax than what had gone hidden before. The reason for this is simple: when it was a hidden tax, various markups were made on top of it, amounting in most cases to around 20%. In other words, *the public, unknowingly, was shelling out up to 25% in taxes on all consumer goods!* Time proved that the GST was, indeed, a more honest tax than had existed previously, but even in these early years of the 21st century, Mulroney continues to be reviled because he made the sales tax visible, rather than hidden. The GST produces so much revenue that in spite of promises to eliminate the tax, rest assured that this tax is here to stay.

The retail business became more competitive than ever with the Wal-Mart chain entry into Canada. Their purchase of the failing Woolco chain gave the American retailing chain, in one fell swoop, full access to most of the cities and towns in Canada.

The Canadian media welcomed their entry into Canada and created the opportunity for Wal-Mart to capitalize on the free advertising. Naturally, Wal-Mart took shrewd advantage of this and, with their proven method of discounting well known brands of merchandise, gave the impression that everything they sold was at a discount. They had a proven format that worked in the United States. Today, Wal-Mart is a world wide phenomena and has grown to be the largest company throughout the world.

Wal-Mart was the forerunner of the "Big Box Chains" which followed to take over the retail business in Canada. There is no question that the Canadian retailers including our three chains, were not prepared for the onslaught. This was a wake up call for all Canadian retailers. You could see the demise of the ones that were not prepared and could not compete. What also became apparent was the absorption of the weaker ones by their larger competitors, i.e. Simpsons by The Bay.

Hard decisions had to be made. There was no question that Gendis management had taken its eyes off the ball; it should have been able to see the dangers lurking just over the border, before they became impossible to remedy. When the losses in the retail business reached $65 million, which had to be absorbed by Gendis, the conclusion that became apparent to the directors at the time, was that Greenbergs, which had absorbed Metropolitan, would have to be placed in receivership. This was a very hard decision that had to be taken.

One thing I made clear to our directors from the very start of our deliberations, was that I wanted to be sure that **not one of our banks would suffer any losses**. Also, anticipating the effect on our suppliers, we would *stop* buying any merchandise for the Christmas season of 1996. This was because we were to make the announcement in February, 1997, that the two chains would be closed.

Consequently, we used the money from our sale of SONY to pay down the debts to the five major banks of Canada. Not a single one of them lost a penny, from the unfortunate but necessary steps we were taking.

In many cases, there were long-term leases at low rental rates in stores we vacated. Landlords were happy to take back their leases without penalty, and were soon able in most cases to lease the properties at higher rental rates. In some cases, because Gendis had guaranteed the leases, it was Gendis who continued to pay the rental, until such time as the landlord could find new tenants, or the leases expired.

One of our directors said something that pleased me, after Gendis had undergone this most traumatic experience in the history of our company:

> *"I believe that there has never been a bankruptcy in the history of Canada, where the banks, the suppliers, and the landlords were all protected by the parent company—namely Gendis—who paid the penalty for the failure."*

In addition, the employees, in most cases, found other jobs, because, as fortune would have it, Canada's business as a whole was booming in the late 1990s. What was Gendis left with? Our principal assets of surplus cash, real estate, and our main asset, the SAAN Store chain, which now numbered some 250 stores. And, most of all, *our good name.*

The Triangle of Success

The principle of the Triangle of Success is simplicity itself. It applies to any product, be it a soft drink like Coca-Cola or to the Chrysler Corporation, which in the late seventies and early eighties *forgot* to use it, and floundered to such an extent that, until they got on track again in 1983, their very existence was threatened.

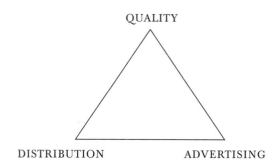

THE TRIANGLE OF SUCCESS

Quality -

The apex of the triangle is a quality product. Paper-Mate had this to offer to the consumer, as does Coca-Cola in its field. (Or at least until that company abandoned and then soon brought back their century-old formula in 1985, this time as Classic Coke). Quality, like Coke, is "it"; without "it," you are dead. Paper-Mate was the best in its field, as it possessed a fast-drying ink which no one else had. It was a big breakthrough to achieve a smooth writing instrument, when all other well-known brand names had failed.

Distribution –

The second point of the triangle is distribution. No matter how good a product is, without proper distribution to make sure that it is visible and easily obtained, the item cannot be successful. Frawley instinctively recognized this, he applied this point to Paper-Mate and even **forced** distribution, to the extent of giving away thousands of pens. He believed in his product, and was confident that the repeats would ensure the success of his venture. In addition, he wisely likened the pen to the Gillette razor. Gillette could afford to give away the razor. Their profit was and still is in the blades. Similarly, Frawley could give away the Paper-Mate pen. His profits were in the millions of refills.

Advertising –

The third point of the triangle is advertising. No matter how good the product or how well distributed, without saturation advertising to inform the public, and extol the virtues of the product, you cannot be successful. Advertising has to cover newspapers, magazines, television which was a new medium in 1952. Frawley sponsored Art Linkletter in the early fifties. The consumer is made aware of the product by advertising, sees it on the shelves and buys the product. Providing the quality is there, he or she becomes the best word-of-mouth advertiser for the manufacturer.

Indeed, word-of-mouth advertising is the most powerful form of all! The consumer will feel a sense of pride and proprietorship in discovering a new product that satisfies his or her needs. They will take pains to extol its virtues to friends and anyone else who will listen.

Being first with a new product is one of the most powerful advantages a manufacturer can have. But care must be taken that the product does not become synonymous with the trademark, as happened with Bayer Aspirin. This brand name became so allied with the headache tablet, that, outside of Canada, Bayer lost the proprietary rights to the brand name "aspirin," and anyone could use it. Nevertheless, because they were first with the product, Bayer's is still the world's largest selling headache tablet.

Another good example of being first with a product is that, Scripto hired Fran Seech away from Frawley and Paper-Mate, thus obtaining the new-formula ink. Even though they put a pen on the market to retail for 98 cents, they were unsuccessful in their efforts to make any inroads on Paper-Mate sales. A further example is that of a pen manufacturer in Chicago, who decided to make a dent in Paper-Mate's sales by designing a very attractive pen with most of the features that had made Paper-Mate successful. One of the silent partners of this pen manufacturer was a well-known executive of an advertising agency. He had the know-how to plan an excellent advertising campaign, with full-page advertisements in *Life* and *Look* magazines, as well as in the newspapers. What he lacked was distribution. His campaign failed, because one point of his triangle was missing, and so the triangle collapsed.

If Chrysler had not seen the error of their ways and the quality of their products, the company would have gone under. They had excellent distribution through their many dealers, and a very good advertising campaign, but their product lacked quality at the time. Once they put quality into their products, the triangle worked for Chrysler.

Any product marketed in the past or that will be marketed in the future must have **all three of the principles of the triangle** working for it, if it is to prove successful. There is no question that the lesson we learned with Paper-Mate was the basis for General Distributors' success with products marketed in the years that followed.

A Honeymoon Takes Me to Japan

As a Canadian involved post-war in developing trade between Japan and Canada, I had the opportunity of viewing as an insider, the emerging giant in world trade and how it happened in such a relatively short time.

General Distributors Ltd., the forerunner of Gendis Inc., an acronym of the name was in the import business with contacts established in the U.S.A. and most of the western European countries. Contacts in Asia were established by mail correspondence primarily in Japan and Hong Kong.

As to how the prime concentration in imports were established in Tokyo therein lies a tale.

As the president and founder of Gendis Inc., it was my responsibility to develop new ideas and make the various contacts to keep the company vibrant and alive in a very competitive business. It necessitated much travel to Europe and many major cities in the U.S.A.

My first trip to the Orient and then to many countries around the world travelling east to west came about in this manner.

Having been a bachelor for most of the years while I was in my twenties and just about when I was beginning to tire of the joys of bachelorhood and the footloose way of life, World War II intervened. By the time the war was over and I had served my time in the Royal Canadian Navy, I was in my middle thirties. Suddenly I was too old for the young attractive interesting girls of the twenties and too young and not too interested in the unmarried women or the alternative divorced or widows available of my age.

Fate intervened in 1951 when I met a young very attractive refugee from Czechoslovakia – Irena Kankova.

Irena who was born in Prague, Czechoslovakia was a brilliant scholar. She achieved the International Baccalaureate at Lycee Francais in Prague. This was followed by a scholarship to study at the Sorbonne in Paris, France.

The U.S.S.R. communists had taken control of Czechoslovakia after the war and had established their puppet regime.

While attending Charles University, Irena became involved in a secret student organization who were working towards an insurrection against the government. As her boyfriend Leopold was the leader of the student group, she became involved with this clandestine organization that came to the attention of the Communist authorities. In the 1950's when the hard Stalinists were in power in Czechoslovakia, there was no room for any democratic movements.

The authorities moved in one evening and arrested the students attending a meeting where plans were being made to form an opposition to the government. Obviously there had been an informer among the students who through coercion or other means had disclosed the meeting place. The students were taken for questioning to the political police station.

At the time Irena was in the theatre as a dancer. She had also been screen tested for the Czech movie studio which was judged highly successful and was slated to be groomed as a starlet. She could have been a stand-in for Audrey Hepburn for whom she was almost a double.

Like most of the well educated Czechs she spoke, read and could write in five languages, French, German, Russian and most of the Slavic languages as well as English. This background made it very easy for her to be the liaison between the student underground groups. Her role was quite minor being just a courier carrying messages between the active participants in the would be opponents to the regime. Being involved in the arts, a pretty attractive young lady who knew how to make the best of her attributes, she was able to move about the city without attracting undue attention.

However, as the student movement became more active, suddenly the political police, in a well coordinated strike, arrested the leaders of the groups. When Leopold was arrested and the names of the students involved became known, Irena was summoned to appear at the police station for questioning. She knew that there was no alternative but to be there at the appointed time. Being young and attractive, as well as an accomplished actress, she was able to convince the authorities to let her go on the understanding that she would return the next day.

Knowing that Leopold and others would, under further forceful interrogation, have to reveal additional names and details of their organization, it was almost certain that she would be arrested the following day.

That evening, at a late night meeting with her parents, it was decided that Irena would escape to West Germany before the authorities would make their next move.

Quickly a knapsack was packed with a few essentials together with some snacks and early the next morning, after bidding her parents a tearful good-bye, she started on a pilgrimage to escape to the west side of Germany where the American sector was located.

Knowing the country side through the many trips her parents had taken her ever since childhood, she kept to seldom traveled paths. At first it was like a walk in the country as she trudged along ever southwest towards the German border. That evening as the sun was setting she came to a farm house. Not knowing how safe it might be as one got closer to the border, many of the farmers were informants and would turn in would be escapees. She decided to spend the night in the barn before proceeding on her way the next morning.

As she was preparing to sleep in a bed of hay, she froze with terror when slowly the barn door opened. The farmer's wife having heard a noise was probably as surprised as she to see this obviously frightened young girl in his barn. On questioning her, she quickly made up a story of being lost and thought that she would be on her way the next morning without disturbing anyone.

Half believing her story she persuaded her to come into the house where she would give her a proper bedding for the night. The farm woman was warm and friendly. After a sound sleep from exhaustion and a hearty breakfast the farmer's wife made up a parcel of food for Irena's continuing journey. It was understood that there would be no questions asked so that there were no answers necessary. In this manner, if the farmers were questioned by the authorities they would have no knowledge of a person seeking to escape across the border.

Her journey, which took her three days, continued to be aided by the hospitality of the farmers along the way providing food and lodging. Finally after spending the last night at a friendly farm she crossed the border at a remote place without incident.

Soon Irena realized she was safe in West Germany. Following several hours of investigation by the nearest unit of the CIC, she was taken to a refugee camp where she told her story. Irena was assured of being permitted to stay until such time as she could emigrate to either Canada or Australia who were permitting immigration under certain conditions. Fortunately she chose Canada where we met in 1951 and were married on November 6, 1953.

Coming from different religions, and cultural backgrounds, most of our friends at the time, now divorced or demised, did not give our marriage much of a chance for success. Irena was an actress, dancer and had been involved in the early years of television while I had some background in the cultural arts and was best known as a moderately successful businessman.

Irena, many years younger than myself, a dancer, actress and one of the early CBC actors in Winnipeg's first T.V. productions soon became well known for her talents. She was chosen to perform the leading role in the Manitoba Theatre Centre production of The Diary of Anne Frank. John Hirsch chose her for the leading role of Anastasia. She was in a number of productions at Rainbow Stage and as well she performed in the leading role of Gigi.

While Irena was visiting her aunt in Denver, The Denver Post did a front-page interview on her escape from Czechoslovakia. The Toronto Star and the Winnipeg Free Press also did similar features. It was understandable for the press at that time to publicize stories of this type of adventure. After all what could be of more interest. A beautiful young girl, an actress, dancer just married to a rising entrepreneur. All this publicity was to come back to haunt us a few years later.

After our marriage we made a brief honeymoon trip to New York. The wonders of the big city which familiar to me, was a joy to show off to my bride. Even the trip on the Staten Ferry to Newark, New Jersey was an adventure to Irena. There is no doubt that this exposure to the freedom of the western world had a great influence on her. It was therefore a surprise to me a few months later when Irena broached the subject to me asking, "When are we going to make the trip around the world that you promised me?" "I don't recall that I ever promised you that. When did I make that promise?" I asked. "Before we were married. Don't you remember?"

Did I promise that I thought. Well, probably I did. After all when you are a bachelor for as many years that I had been and courting a beautiful young dancer, actress, I probably did promise. Next scene as the head of an import firm, with Irena acting as my secretary and girl Friday, we set off to see the world.

MR. AND MRS. ALBERT D. COHEN, Colonial house apartments, left Thursday afternoon by air to embark on a round-the-world trip. They will spend a week in Beverly Hills, Calif. prior to leaving for the Far East, visiting Hawaii, Tokyo, Hong Kong, Rangoon, Bankok, Delhi, Calcutta, Tel Aviv, Istanbul, and the following European countries, Greece, Italy, Switzerland, Spain, France and England. They will be away three months.

Article from the Winnipeg Free Press; June, 1954.

It was in June 1954 that my wife Irena and I started a round the world trip that took us from Winnipeg to seventeen different countries before our return three months later.

Irena and I boarded a Trans Canada Airlines plane, beginning a trip that was to take us to many countries over a period of three months. After brief stays in Los Angeles (where we were royally entertained by the Frawleys and Ettingers) and Hawaii, we flew on to Tokyo. We checked into the fabled old Imperial Hotel, a low-slung hostelry magnificently designed by Frank Lloyd Wright to withstand all of Japan's major earthquakes, and then strode down to the Ginza to get our first sight and feel of that crowded city. The bustling, jostling mass of Japanese humanity was overwhelming. Because Irena was so self-reliant, we arranged that for the rest of our stay in Japan I would go about my business contacts during the day, and she would site-see on her own. We would meet for dinner and see the city together, an arrangement which worked fine. Irena had an assignment to write an article for *Dance Magazine* of New York, and I arranged to meet with suppliers that I had known only through correspondence.

I discovered that, because of the language difficulty, I was unable to make any new contacts. Fortunately, a mutual friend had given me a contact, a Mr. Harvey Brotman, who was in the export business and living in Tokyo.

I had not intended to call on Brotman. I knew his services would entail a commission on anything I bought through him, but I soon saw that it was hopeless to try and make a go of it alone, so I contacted him on the third day after our arrival in Tokyo.

Brotman was a man of about fifty years of age, and what was known as an "Old Japanese Hand," denoting the fact that he had spent a long time in Asia, and knew his way around. His wife, Eva, was a charming woman, who took an immediate liking to Irena. In short order we became good friends. I engaged Brotman's services on the basis of a 3 per cent commission to be paid on any items purchased through his contacts.

This was important in many ways. If something was wrong with merchandise that I was importing from Japan, I would have to "go back" for a credit. They were honourable, and I always would get the credit, but one could not recover everything, so I needed Brotman to handle things on that side of the world. I established a Letter of Credit, but before it could be drawn upon in Japan, there was to be a Letter of Inspection. This meant that people in the country of origin would have to do a spot check on the merchandise, and could not receive that Letter of Credit until they remedied the problem. This way, when merchandise finally came into Canada, it had already been checked, which allowed us to eliminate a lot of problems so endemic at the time. Thus, we were able to often put our own brand name on the products, which is how we truly started to build the various companies. Yes, our merchandise was coming out of Japan, but they stood up, where so many other importers could not make that claim. We paid extra money, alright, but we got quality goods.

Brotman had an office in the Fukoku Building, just a block away from the Imperial Hotel. He employed a staff of five, and his right hand man was Frank Wertheimber. Frank, a very interesting person, was born of a German father and a Japanese mother. He was thin with angular features, a pencil mustache, and stood six feet tall, which was towering for a Japanese, especially in those days before their diet of rice and fish had changed so much to bread and meat. The modern Japanese is much taller than his counterpart of the early fifties.

Frank spoke many languages fluently. He was born in Yokohama and educated at St. Joseph Catholic School. Drafted into the army in 1937, he served in the Cavalry of the Emperor's Royal Household Guards in Manchuria. Because of his linguistic ability, he also served as an interpreter throughout the war. Captured by the Soviets near the end of the Pacific war, he soon became proficient in the Russian language as well. This was the background of this most interesting person, whom I came to know so well. The Japanese who did not know him thought he was a foreigner, while Americans, and others such as myself, thought Frank looked Japanese.

It soon became apparent that the move to employ Brotman and his facilities was the right one. Many fresh contacts were made, and the range of products we imported from Japan was greatly enlarged. I visited many factories with Wertheimber, and, because in most cases the owners spoke no English, Wertheimber was invaluable as an interpreter. I even had a meeting with Toyota, to discuss bringing their cars to Canada long before the western world was aware of the quality of their product.

Frank lived in Yokohama with his wife and two young sons. Every day, he would travel for an hour, by crammed commuter train, to his office in Tokyo. One of the things that surprised me was how Harvey Brotman would make snide remarks about the Japanese in Frank's presence. I knew that Frank must have been hurt by these remarks, but he never showed any emotion. When the opportunity arose, I asked Brotman why he spoke this way. His offhand remark was, "I want to keep him in his place", this was his way of doing it. I felt that Brotman showed a lack of sensitivity, and I was repelled by his attitude.

One evening, Irena's eyes were opened to the fact that Japan was very much a man's world. The president of Kanto Optical Manufacturing, a supplier of binoculars we had been importing for a number of years, invited us for dinner at the Imperial Hotel. I had never met the owner before this trip, and discovered that it was the custom for Japanese to entertain their customers lavishly whenever they could. Part of the reason for this was that, although salaries were quite low, expenses for entertainment were recognized as a necessity, and consequently never questioned by the Japanese tax authorities. Without this generous interpretation of the law, it is doubtful whether the many hundreds of restaurants, bars and geisha houses could have existed.

When we met Mr. Kubota, when we appeared at the appointed time, he had his secretary with him. It is seldom that a Japanese businessman would entertain outside of his home with his wife in attendance. At least that is how it was in the fifties and sixties, and today, probably, this custom has changed to some extent. If you were held in the highest regard, you would be invited to a Japanese home to meet the wife and family.

Another surprise was that Mr. Kubota hardly spoke a word of English. Even though our correspondence had been carried on for years, I found that Miss Fumi, his secretary, who was a Nisei, born in Hawaii, was responsible for the good grammar, so different from some of the fractured English letters we would get from some of our other suppliers.

When we were ushered into the dining room where Mr. Kubota had reserved our table, Irena was surprised when no attention was paid to her. Mr. Kubota held my chair for me to be seated, and the conversation was carried on through our interpreter, which was mostly about our business relationship. Finally, after a lengthy dialogue, Miss Fumi, with many a giggle, and with her hand before her face, declared, "Mr. Kubota says that Mr. Cohen - heh, heh, heh - next time you come to Japan - heh, heh, heh - come alone, do not bring wife, you will have much better time - heh, heh, heh." Neither saw anything wrong with making this statement, as he felt he was just giving me good advice, and both Irena and I have had many a laugh over our dinner experience at the Imperial Hotel as guests of Mr. Kubota.

Later on, as the years went by, and after my innumerable trips to Japan, I could understand the reason for the Japanese economic miracle that so stunned the world over the next few decades, in spite of the extreme sexism that we encountered on that 1954 honeymoon trip. The people were single-minded in their devotion to their jobs, no matter how menial: even if it was workmen repairing streets, there was no leaning on shovels, as often seen in the West. Working in the fields or in the factories, there was an intense interest in accomplishment, and in the quality of work.

Toward the end of our journey, an old friend of mine, Colonel John Allan, who had been put in command of Supply and Services for the Canadian Armed Forces during the Korean War, made a remark that may have influenced to a great extent my thinking about the Japanese. At the time, the Japanese reputation worldwide was as producers of shoddy merchandise. A recent Internet-spread list of "You Know You're Getting Older If. . . ." had a good line: *"You Know You're Getting Older If You Remember When 'Made in Japan' Meant Junk."* Most of the items, whether toys, lighters, optical goods or clothing, were cheaply priced and did not stand up to wear and tear.

John told me over brandy at the Grand Hotel in Osaka, that he had been surprised to discover the high quality of the products that he purchased for the Canadian Army in the early 1950s. Whereas he had first thought that he would have to import cameras and binoculars from Germany, the prime source of quality optical goods at the time, he had found two companies, Canon and Nikon, to be producers of cameras every bit as good or better than the finest German brands. Reporters and photographers from the U.S. and Canada had discovered this, and were buying Japanese cameras in preference to the German Leica, which had been the camera most in demand until then. John suggested that I visit the various department stores and see the exceptional state-of-the-art products on sale, products that we had never seen up to that time in the West.

Of course, it took a while and many years of superior Japanese craftsmanship and successful exporting for the rest of the world to recognize the Japanese gift for excellence in consumer products. Later, I brought back some stunning "Made in Japan" watches back from our trip around the world, and showed them to my friend Gerstein at Peoples Credit Jewelers, when we had returned to Canada.

"We sell Bulova!" he brushed me off. *"Who's going to be interested in a Japanese watch?"*

How times would change, within a few short years. In my own case, Japanese expertise would become the nucleus of the growth of a small Canadian import company at that time, known as General Distributors Ltd., with a worth of $35,000 in 1954, to Gendis Inc. today, a public company listed on the Toronto Stock Exchange.

Our James Bond Episode in Prague

It was in 1961 that Irena, upon a visit to her recently widowed mother in Czechoslovakia, was briefly held by the police as "an enemy of the state," because of the newspaper articles written about her over a decade earlier, in which she had maligned the communist government.

I had visited Prague, Czechoslovakia, on December 16, 1960 and established trade contacts with export officials. I decided, in retrospect, foolishly, that it would be safe now to have Irena reunited with her mother and other members of her family. One day, while speaking to my friend Ian Fleming, I mentioned our plans to visit Prague. He advised me that even with the liberalization of the new Dubcek regime, this could still be a very dangerous venture for Irena. I, therefore, contacted the Czech Legation in Ottawa to make sure that there would be no problems if Irena and Anthony, who was not quite three years of age, accompanied me to Prague.

We intended to spend about three weeks in July visiting with her mother, and aunt and uncle Charles, who was a professor teaching medicine at Charles University. The officials at the Legation assured me that there would be no problems as long as I obtained an entrance and exit visa. I was assured that the Czech government had declared an amnesty for political refugees and as long as no criminal offence had been committed, there would be no problem in Irena visiting her mother and relatives. The visas were received in due time and the three of us embarked for Prague.

We arrived August 17, 1961 and there was a very emotional reunion between Irena and her mother at the Airport. We then proceeded to the Alcron Hotel where the concierge, who recognized me from my trip the previous December, greeted us warmly. As was customary, I left our two passports with the concierge and was to pick them up the following morning once we had been duly reported to the police as to our whereabouts.

That evening we dined at the hotel and I listened patiently as I did not understand a word of the eager conversation between mother and daughter to bring each other up to date for the interval of twelve years since they had seen each other. Anthony stayed with his grandmother that evening and Irena and I arranged that we would meet the next morning for breakfast and then go on a sightseeing trip around the city.

The next morning, after breakfast, we proceeded to see the sights, visiting famous Hradcany Castle, the Art Gallery, various squares and all the places that tourists usually frequent. I had warned Irena to wear clothes as drab as she had available, otherwise she would stand out as a curiosity in this unsmiling politically-oppressed society. Even so, we could not help noticing how people turned and stared at us curiously, as westerners were not too much in evidence in those restrictive travel days.

When we returned to the Alcron later in the day, and I called at the desk for our passports, I was dumbfounded to find that my passport had been returned, but to my grave concern, Irena's had not. Instead there was a note ordering her to report to the police station at 8:00 a.m. the following morning. It was evident that we were in for some nasty trouble. Without telling Mrs. Kankova, Irena's mother, that there was anything wrong, I asked her to take care of Anthony the next morning as Irena and I had to visit the Canadian Legation.

When we were alone in our room, I put my fingers to my lips, got some paper and wrote a note to Irena, saying that we should communicate in this manner, not only would our telephone be bugged, but our room also, in all probability. Having noticed a telephone booth in the lobby of the hotel, I would try to contact the assistant to the Canadian Minister, Ted Arcand, with whom I had become acquainted on my previous trip. Fortunately, I was able to reach him.

"Ted, I think we are in trouble." I told him the problem and read out the order to report to the police station.

"You are in serious trouble," Ted replied. "That is the address of the political police."

"Ted, I'm calling you from the telephone booth in the Alcron Hotel. Is it safe to talk?"

"They're probably listening to every word we are saying, so it doesn't matter. Why do you think they kept your wife's passport?"

I then related in detail, Irena's story, her work as a student activist against the communist government; her flight from Czechoslovakia in 1949; her interviews in the Toronto Star, Winnipeg Free Press and Denver Post which had featured her negative reports on the oppressive communist rule in Czechoslovakia.

"Didn't you realize that all these interviews would be sent to Ottawa and then on to Prague, to be placed in a file, to be used against her someday?"

"But I was assured in Ottawa by the Czech Legation that all political refugees had been pardoned." I replied.

"Don't report to the police station tomorrow morning. I'll meet you at 8:30 a.m. and we will proceed together. I'll try to do the best I can for you."

My heart sank on hearing Arcand's doubts about the return of Irena's passport. In checking my own passport, the following message was clearly stated inside the cover:

WARNING

Canadian citizens born abroad, or whose parents were born abroad, are warned that they may be considered by the governments of the countries of their origin or birth to be nationals of these countries, although by Canadian law they are citizens of Canada. They should bear in mind, therefore, that when they are within the boundaries of these countries, it may not be possible for Canada to give them effective protection.

DEPARTMENT OF EXTERNAL AFFAIRS   OTTAWA 1959

Furthermore, Anthony was listed in her passport, as is the case with minors. I tried not to show my anxiety when I reported the conversation with Arcand. Irena, however, had a pretty good idea of the problems involved as she recognized the address where we were to report as the same as where she had been interrogated prior to her escape to Germany.

The next morning Arcand arrived and we had a quick conference. "Albert," he said, "Whatever you do, don't let them separate you from Irena, even when she is taken into the office to be interrogated. If necessary, force your way into the office. Otherwise you may never see your wife again."

"Why is that?"

"Because they have a series of adjoining offices with connecting doors on each side. You may see her go in one office, but they can quickly shift her through a maze of adjoining offices, so we may never know her whereabouts."

We waited, speaking softly. Suddenly, a rough looking character wearing an open tie-less shirt appeared around the office door and beckoned Irena to follow him. I immediately rose to accompany her but he indicated with a rough gesture to wait outside. He spoke to Irena in Czech, which Arcand understood. Arcand explained that I was Irena's husband and both he and I pushed our way into the office. As our voices were raised, immediately the two doors on each of the side walls swung open and policemen with rifles stood ready. The officer motioned them away and the doors were closed.

After a lengthy conversation in Czech, Irena informed me that the police were accusing her of being "an enemy of the state" because of the articles which had been printed in the foreign press maligning the Czech government. She explained that she had been a young student and all she had done was carry messages for her boyfriend at the time.

Arcand translated for me. "I want you to know I called on your Legation in Ottawa. They granted us entrance and exit visas. Don't you honour your country's pledges?"

"We don't care what that Department of External Affairs of government says or does. We have our own rules", he replied. The arguments went on for well over an hour.

Finally, Arcand said, "Mrs. Cohen's passport does not belong to her. It is the property of the Canadian government. Unless you return the passport at once, I will have my minister call your prime minister. I want you to return the passport at once."

The official glared at Arcand, and if looks could kill, Ted would have dropped on the spot. Finally he opened a drawer, withdrew the passport and threw it across the desk saying, "You have twenty-four hours to get out of the country."

We hurried out to Arcand's station wagon. Arcand said, "You're not out of this yet. Albert, I'm going to take Irena to the Canadian Legation as I don't trust the police. They may try to take her into custody at the Alcron or the airport. We have a Canadian citizen born in Czechoslovakia who returned for a visit. He was arrested on a similar charge and sentenced to seven years in prison. We have been endeavouring for months to get him released without success. Therefore, we should take absolutely no chances with Irena. She will be safe at the Legation and I would recommend that you go back to the Alcron, pack your bags and we will arrange a plane booking to get you out of the country."

After leaving Irena at the Canadian Legation, Arcand and I drove to the hotel. Sure enough, the bully boys were already there lounging in the lobby. They did not bother me, but I am sure would have taken Irena into custody if she had been there with me.

I had to break the news to Irena's mother that we had to leave the country at once. It was heartbreaking as this was turning out to be a twenty-four hour visit. The concierge looked curious. "Leaving already?"

I said, "Yes, by request of the secret police".

He answered, "Maybe you are better off."

This sounded as if he regretted that he was not in a position to leave the country even if he wanted to.

After our return to the Legation, Mrs. Kankova insisted on coming with us to say goodbye. She said, "I don't care what they do with me. I'm an old lady already."

Arcand arranged a booking to Vienna on Czech Airlines that was leaving at 6:00 p.m. He said this would be reported and the police would probably be there to make sure we left the country. He then found out that Air France would be coming in from Warsaw, and would depart for Paris at 5:00 p.m.

"I'll drive you to the airport and we will see if I can get you booked on this flight." At 3:30 we left in his station wagon lying down in the back so we would not be seen. The police were watching the Legation and we were taking no chances.

On arrival at the airport, which fortunately was very crowded, a harassed official looked at our passports, looked us over carefully, then after some hesitation stamped our exit visas.

The Air France plane arrived. After a tearful goodbye to Mrs. Kankova, the three of us walked out to the plane accompanied by Arcand, who used his ministerial privileges, as he did not feel we were out of danger.

Before we could board the Caravelle, armed soldiers went through the plane to make sure there were no stowaways. Only then were we permitted to board. On board, waiting for the plane to take off, suddenly I was asked to step off the plane. I did not know what to expect as Irena looked at me with apprehension. When I descended to the tarmac, I was approached by an attendant who said, "Your luggage is overweight and you owe an additional twenty dollars". I gladly paid him the amount and was allowed to re-board the plane.

Once the plane took off, it only took an hour for us to land at Orly Airport in Paris. When we arrived at the George Cinq Hotel and were settled in our room and the full impact of what we had been through struck Irena, only then did the tears begin to flow.

Place:	Hotel de la Borda
	Taxco, Mexico
Time:	September 4, 1957
Poem:	Dedicated to three offspring not yet born:
	Anthony, James and Anna-Lisa
Inspired by:	Ian Fleming, Author and friend of Albert D. Cohen

THE FEMALE SPY

Who is the pretty millionairess
Sipping coffee on the terrace
On the table gladiolus
Beneath the terrace strum violas
Here in Taxco's silver mountains
Near the purple reddish fountain
The sun is shining on the houses
Women wear colorful blouses
Brilliant sky is high and blue
Chihuahuas howl, there are a few
The smithy's hammer silver pieces
To delight the tourist species
More than wealth, here is peace
Solitude sets mind at ease
She feels magic in the air
Enchantment that is truly rare
Soothing broken heart and soul
Here at last she's found her goal
She would rest, she's travelled far
SECRET ORDERS - ZANZIBAR

| Verse by: | Irena Kankova Cohen |
| Assisted by: | Albert D. Cohen |

Opportunity Knocks in Japan

As Japan was beginning to rebuild and take over from the American occupation forces, they were rescinding some of the privileges afforded to Americans. The new rules placed all foreigners, for tax purposes, on the same footing as Japanese citizens, the reason for Brotman closing his operations in Japan. I arranged to meet with him in Honolulu to discuss our takeover of his office and staff.

On September 15, 1955, Irena and I boarded a Canadian Pacific flight for Honolulu. The plane stopped in Calgary, and I was surprised to have brother Harry meet me at the airport. He breathlessly told me the news which had come over the Dow Jones, to the effect that Pat Frawley was negotiating the sale of Paper-Mate to Eversharp Inc. This was most disconcerting to hear. I presumed that Frawley would have advised me if he was in negotiation for the sale of the company. *What if he did not keep his promise about leaving Canada in the hands of General Distributors?* His company was central to our present success, and our very survival, much less growth!

The next stop was Vancouver, where brother Joe met me and told me that there was a further rumour in the air: Paper-Mate was in the process of being sold to Gillette Inc.! I called Pat Frawley in Los Angeles to ask him if there was any truth to the rumours. He reassured me by saying that there was nothing final and that he was still in negotiations. I advised him that I was on my way to Japan, but that I would stop in Los Angeles in about a month's time, so he could bring me up to date. I concluded our conversation by reminding him of his promise to protect our interests in the distribution of Paper-Mate in Canada. He gave me his assurance of this once more, but I felt uneasy, as it was obvious that he had been negotiating the sale of Paper-Mate for the past few months in secret. He should have at least kept me informed of what was going on. Was this why he insisted on buying back my stock in Paper-Mate Eastern?

On our arrival in Honolulu, we were met by Harvey and Eva Brotman at the airport. Over dinner at their apartment, Harvey told me that they had purchased a gift shop in Honolulu and had already taken up residence in Waikiki, commuting each day to their store. It was arranged that I would take over his office and staff of five employees. I bought his assets, which consisted of some office furniture, and assumed his lease, which had about a year to run. He arranged to phone Wertheimber to advise him that I would be arriving within a few days. That weekend, I left Irena at the Surfrider Hotel and promised that I would be back from Tokyo in about two weeks. When I arrived at the Haneda Airport, Wertheimber was there to greet me. He welcomed the new arrangements and assured me of his full assistance and cooperation.

Every morning, Wertheimber would come to Tokyo by train from his home in Yokohama, an hour trip on a train in which the passengers were packed like sardines. The first thing I felt I should do was have the company buy an automobile for Frank. When I told him of this, he was overwhelmed, because he was not used to this consideration and treatment. Wertheimber bought a Toyota, which at the time cost less than $2,000. As early as 1955, I was quite surprised by the quality of the automobiles that the Japanese manufacturers were producing. The streets were crowded with vehicles, with taxis in abundance, and everyone used them because of the extremely low fares. I was also surprised to find that when I wanted to tip the driver, he firmly returned the yen tendered; it was not their custom. Frank pleaded with me, "Please, Mr. Cohen," he would never call me by anything but my surname, "Don't spoil it for us. The service people here in the hotels and taxi drivers do not expect or accept tips." How refreshing, I thought. I tried to remember, but like many westerners, I would often forget, and would just as often be rebuffed by the refusal of my proffered tips.

During the weeks I spent in Tokyo, Frank would join me every morning for breakfast at the Imperial Hotel to bring me up to date on events that he read about in the Japanese newspapers. I would usually read the *Nippon Times,* the morning English newspaper. On this particular morning, a small news item caught my attention. It related that a firm by the name of Tokyo Tsushin Kogyo Ltd. had produced the first transistor radio - the TR55. I asked Frank to phone the company and make an appointment, as I was most curious to see this item.

General Distributors, at this time in its history, had been involved in importing many products, and I was responsible for all the buying. I had some knowledge of the products we were importing, but no expert on any one product. My first connection with radios was on a trip to Chicago in 1939, when I had tracked down a small manufacturer of a four-tube portable radio named Silver and Co. I purchased seventy-two radios and imported them into Calgary. They were attractive, and we eventually sold them, but I saw no possibility in developing a market for this item. The radio functioned on an expensive "B" battery, together with three "C" batteries. They didn't last more than a few days, and often the tubes burned out. In addition, it was difficult to get replacement tubes.

The second experience was when we imported and sold one thousand radios through Tsurumi Trading Co. of Tokyo. These were purchased on my first trip to Japan in 1954. They were of better quality, but the radio essentially had the same problems: expensive batteries and tubes that had to be replaced often. The product, although low in price, was less than satisfactory.

In the previous two years, I had read quite a few articles about a new invention, the transistor. These had appeared in *Fortune* magazine, *The Wall Street Journal, Business Week,* and other periodicals that I considered as "must reading" to keep abreast of the new technologies and everyday business activity.

THE PHENOMENON OF "BEING AWARE" OF HAVING

ONE'S SENSES WORKING AT SHARPEST PITCH

THE SOUND OF OPPORTUNITY KNOCKING WAS

HAPPENING AT THIS PRECISE TIME!

Wertheimber returned to the breakfast table and told me that he had made contact with Tokyo Tsushin Kogyo Ltd. and we were to see them at 2:00 p.m. that afternoon. Their factory was located in the Shinagawa district, about a fifteen-minute ride from the hotel. At the time I thought no more about it. This was just another appointment, one of many that we made from day-to-day, and I have the happy facility of being able to concentrate on whatever I happen to be doing at that particular time. The calls we made that morning had to have my full and undivided attention.

Later, we lunched at the Imperial Hotel and then went on to our 2:00 appointment. The office of the company was in an old wooden house most unpretentious. We asked a young lady to tell the manager that we had arrived.

On exchange of business cards, I saw that the young man was named M. Naruse. He spoke reasonable English, but so that there would be no misunderstanding, Wertheimber related in Japanese the background of General Distributors, and our interest in the new product mentioned in the newspaper story. Mr. Naruse advised us that the radio had not been marketed as yet, and that the story in the press was probably premature, but he agreed to show me the radio. He left the room and soon reappeared.

I was impressed first of all with the small size of the TR55—so named because it was invented in 1955. It measured only 5 " x 3 " x 1 1/4 " the smallest portable I had ever seen. When I turned on the switch, the music came through loud and clear. I removed the back and found that it operated on the strength of only four penlight batteries and five transistors. When I asked Naruse what was the life of the batteries, he said they would last up to six months or longer, as the power drain was ever so light, due to the transistors. I was impressed, but when I asked what the export price of the radio would be, Naruse answered that *they had not contemplated exporting* the radio, but that the price would be about $27 each. This shocked me, as by rapid calculation of three times the FOB price, I knew the radio would have to sell for $79.95 to the Canadian consumer. To pay the various duties, sales tax, excise tax, ocean cargo, rail transportation, insurance, brokerage charges, then the various markups, it was necessary to calculate a three times mark-up on the FOB price.

However, rather than reject the radio as not saleable, in view of the experience with Paper-Mate, I decided to pursue this further. After all, I reasoned, the public could buy a pen which looked similar to Paper-Mate for one-third the price, yet we were selling almost one million pens a year. You could buy a bottle of ink for 15 cents, yet we were selling two million Paper-Mate refills annually at 69 cents each. Price, then, was not a factor, as people will always pay for quality and convenience. *Perhaps this radio, because of its small size and because it operated on four inexpensive penlight batteries, might be marketed successfully as a new item for our company?*

I shall note here that as I write these words early in 2002, I have a TR55 sitting on my desk in Winnipeg, which still operates, nearly a half-century later. And there is another one in the Smithsonian Museum in Washington, D.C.

I asked Naruse if I might take the radio back to the hotel with me, to test out its quality. He agreed, and we made arrangements to meet again in two days. I asked him to discuss with his superiors the possibilities of a lower price for export purposes, and he agreed to check this out and would give me an answer at our next meeting.

That evening, back in my room, I tried out the transistor radio. The Imperial Hotel's walls were very thick, and the reception had been extremely poor with the portable tube radio that I had brought with me. When I turned on the switch of the TR55, I was amazed to hear the reception loud and clear! The new transistor radio worked beautifully, and brought in station after station. I decided to leave the radio on, through the night. The next morning, it was still going strong, with no perceptible loss of power. I felt that this was an item with great potential for increasing volume for General Distributors.

At our next appointment, Mr. Naruse arranged me to meet with a man named Akio Morita, the general manager of the tiny firm. **This was the moment in which the direction of our company was to be influenced for all time. This was the product I had been searching for, throughout the world, which would finally catapult a small, family-owned import company to one of the foremost merchandising companies in Canada.**

OPPORTUNITY WAS KNOCKING

SO VERY FAINTLY AT MY DOOR,

AND I HAD RECOGNIZED THE SOUND!

Masuru Ibuka and Akio Morita, co-founders of SONY Corporation Tokyo, Japan.

The Men Who Created SONY

Masaru Ibuka, as I was later to discover, was a genius of a man who was educated as a physicist, engineer and inventor all combined in a modest rather reclusive personality.

In the 1986, 40th Anniversary of the SONY Management Newsletter, Yuzuru Tanigawa, a close friend and neighbor related this episode of when he was a young student. One day on the way to school, he was passing Ibuka's home when he was surprised to see him on the roof of his home. Unobserved, he stopped to see Ibuka busily moving about and he wondered what he was up to.

Both Tanigawa and Ibuka were born in Kobe, a seaport city some distance from Tokyo. On making his presence known, Ibuka informed him in confidence that he was trying to find a place to hide his roof antenna so that a government inspector would not discover it. The government made it known that there would be a severe penalty if anyone without a license was caught listening to a program.

It was in March 1925 that Japan's first experimental radio broadcast was transmitted from Tokyo. This was the signal that Ibuka was trying to capture. Ibuka through devious ways as a young student, had been able to scrape up three vacuum tubes. He then had constructed a radio receiver. Ever the innovator, he found out by experiment that by placing a rice bowl upside down over the receiver he could amplify the sound. This was probably the first attempt at inventing that gave Ibuka the desire to continue his studies in the field of radio and electricity. It was not long after that he became interested in short wave and became a HAM operator communicating with other HAM friends throughout the Kobe, Osaka and Tokyo area.

From this time when Ibuka and Tanigawa started to receive call letters from other HAM operators throughout Japan information was exchanged and a friendship developed which in future years their paths would cross many times.

It was around this time that Ibuka was busy studying for his college entrance exams. He was successful and was admitted by Waseda University in Tokyo. For a time though through this experience he learned much about electricity which he explored so successfully throughout his lifetime.

In 1933, prior to graduating from Waseda, Ibuka took the employment examination for Toshiba, but he failed. Later, with the help of a friend, he found his first job with the Photo-Chemical Laboratory (PCL).

"You may do whatever you want to do. So why won't you come and work for my company?" President Taiji Uemura said to Masaru Ibuka. Rejected by Toshiba, his first choice, Ibuka highly appreciated and quickly took up Mr. Uemura's offer. Though PCL was a small company, Ibuka especially liked the idea of being allowed to do his individual research there.

When studying in the Engineering Faculty of Waseda University, Ibuka conducted extensive research on optical modulation – the means of modulating light by sound or external voltage. He invented a "running neon" device which utilized the physical property of light to expand and contract whenever a high frequency electric current changed its frequency in a neon tube. While conventional neon lights were made only to shine statically, Ibuka's "running neon" light was so designed to look like it moved dynamically inside the tube. The brilliant device earned him a patent while he was still in college. Ibuka submitted many inventions and ingenious ideas to the Patent Office and came to be known as an outstanding student inventor. After starting work at PCL, Ibuka submitted his "running neon" device to the International Expo in Paris and got an award for excellent merit.

Ibuka, with his own professional interest in sound recording, began to worry about his future when PCL became a full-fledged movie production company. He talked to Mr. Uemura and got transferred to the radio department of Nihon Ko-on an affiliate established in 1937 to produce 16-mm sound motion picture projectors.

After a while, Ibuka became dissatisfied with his work in Nihon Ko-on's radio department. His idea was to make the radio department of Nihon Ko-on an independent company specializing in measuring instruments and asked Nihon Ko-on to make the capital investment. Thus in the fall of 1940, Ibuka's new company, the Japan Precision Instrument Co. (Nissoku) was established with Masaru Ibuka as Managing Director.

Nissoku also did work for the army and the navy, as Ibuka was acquainted with many engineers working in their technical laboratories. They valued Ibuka's talent highly, and before too long the main business of Nissoku became filling their orders.

The first major work in this line was a unique frequency selection relay invented by Ibuka. Ensuring easy selection of several frequencies, this device made it possible to modulate a very low frequency into a high frequency wave and amplify the modulated frequency by interrupting the low frequency wave at this contact point. Inevitably, this idea and its military application were utilized.

The Navy first saw the value of this new technology as a practical means of detecting enemy submarines. As the war worsened, many students were mobilized for wartime production and were sent to Nissoku's Tsukishima factory, among them female students from the Music Academy in Ueno.

Around this time Ibuka attended meetings of the Wartime Research Committee that studied new weapons.

The Wartime Research Committee, through which Ibuka met Morita, was conducting extensive urgent research on new, sophisticated electric wave and electron weaponry in order to recover the Japanese advantage in the war. Akio Morita had graduated as an engineer, and upon enlistment in the navy, he was appointed a lieutenant. Ibuka came to like this young naval lieutenant's candor and intelligence, while Morita was attracted to Ibuka's personality and engineering insight. The two men naturally became intimate friends, though Ibuka was more than a dozen years older.

Ibuka had known for a long time that the war was going to end. Having resolved to move to Tokyo after the end of the war, Ibuka began to map out his postwar plan of action. Then, in 1945, defeat became reality.

After the defeat of Japan, Ibuka opened a small company to repair radios in some space he had rented in a bombed-out department store. He began with seven workers—his "seven Samurai" as he called them. Somewhat of a dreamer, Ibuka was an able, inventive genius and anxious to have Morita join him in establishing a company that would develop new products for demands that would follow the rebirth of Japan after the war. He had been very impressed with Morita's unbounded enthusiasm and vitality. At this time, Morita was employed as a lecturer at the Tokyo Institute of Technology. In his spare time, he would drop in and offer advice to Ibuka in his new venture, but he resisted the inventor's entreaties to join him.

It was in 1946 that Douglas MacArthur issued an order banning former military officers, as well as top executives of the Zaibatsu, from holding public office. This forced Morita to give up his job lecturing at the national university.

With the future looking brighter, Ibuka decided to incorporate. For this, he was keen to have Morita join him.

Akio Morita was the eldest son of a 300 year old sake brewing family. He had the responsibility of taking over his family business. Ibuka realized that it would be difficult to ask the elder Kyuzaemon Morita to consent to his son's partnership with him so Ibuka convinced his father-in-law, Maeda, to join him on a trip to Kisugaya to see him. A meeting was arranged with Morita senior, at which the father listened impassively to Ibuka's entreaties to have Akio join his company as a partner. Kyuzaemon Morita still hoped to lure his eldest son to carry on the centuries-old brewing tradition of the family, but Akio was strong willed and mercurial. He wanted to prove himself. He could not see himself tied to his moderate sized, family owned enterprise. He was impatient to go on to greater things, and felt strongly that Ibuka had the genius to develop the products that would find a ready market in Japan.

"My son should do what he likes best. I wish your company the best of luck, and I hope you all work hard," said Kyuzaemon, without much hesitation, as he warmly received the visitors from Tokyo. He even told Ibuka to come and see him any time the company had problems. Ibuka was so relieved. It was also a great help to have Kazuaki, Akio's younger brother, volunteer to carry on the Morita family's sake brewery.

The problem then was capitalization. Ibuka was an excellent manager when handling new technologies, but was not so skilled in managing money matters. Neither was Maeda. Maeda sought the advice of Mr. Michiharu Tajima, a close friend from his university days and a former director of the Monetary Control Association during the war. He had many influential connections in financial circles. "My son-in-law is starting a company, and he needs capital. I wonder if you could approach your bank connections?" Maeda asked his friend. "Who will be your partner?" Tajima asked Ibuka. "Morita," replies Ibuka. "Morita is good," said Tajima, who had known the Moritas very well during the long time he worked for Aichi Bank. Tajima readily consented, agreeing to act as advisor to the young company.

Tajima sought among his banker friends someone who would be interested in fostering such a company. He turned to and managed to acquire financing from President Junshiro Bandai of the Imperial Bank (now Mitsui Bank).

The company had three internal supervisors: the former Minister of Education, Maeda; Tajima, who later became Director of the Imperial Household Agency' and Mr. Rim Masutani, who had supported Ibuka both materially and morally since his PCL days. It also had two external advisors: Bandai, former Chairman of Japan Bankers Association; and Kyuzaemon Morita, Akio's father. Blessed with those five prominent supporters, drawn from the upper political and economic echelons of Japanese society, Tokyo Tsushin Kogyo (Tokyo Telecommunications Engineering Corporation), with some 20 members and capital of 190,000 yen, was ready for its official inauguration. The capital was borrowed, not from the bank, but from all the workers. Possessing only their brains and engineering know-how, the men set about opening new markets. Their own creativity and innovation would be their sole guide down paths untrodden

The small company had made its start. "With its superior technologies and spirit of perfect unity, it will grow. As it does, we can certainly make a contribution to society." With that statement by Ibuka, Tokyo Tsushin Kogyo Kabushiki Kaisha (Tokyo Telecommunications Engineering Corporation, or Totsuko was born on May 7, 1946. Masaru Ibuka was 38 and Akio Morita was 25.

One of Ibuka's first customers was the Japan Broadcasting Company (NHK), which purchased high quality studio consoles and gave the company some seed money. Then, he and Morita brainstormed for other products to develop for sale to the slowly recovering Japanese economy.

In the true sense of an entrepreneur, when Ibuka was shown a military tape recorder by an official of the Civil Information and Education Services of the Occupation Forces, he became intrigued with this new technology. Not only was the product new, but if Totsuko made a similar product, they would have to produce the *tape* for the recorder, as well. As synthetics to produce tape were not available, Ibuka had to produce a magnetic paper tape of such quality that the tape transport would not snag. After much experiments, he became successful.

This became a topsy-turvy tradition: Totsuko manufactured the product; now a demand had to be created. This pattern would be repeated with transistor radios, videocassette machines, the Walkman, and countless other inspired SONY products over the next half-century. With true genius for salesmanship, Ibuka and Morita bought a truck and toured schools throughout the country, demonstrating their new creation and showing the innovative use of the recorder for educational purposes. They were successful in selling sufficient quantities to generate funds for further development of their tape technology.

As Totsuko's tape recorder technology grew, Ibuka decided to make his first trip to the US to see if he could make headway for his product in that huge school market. He had heard of the development of the transistor by Bell Laboratories, but did not at that time relate the possibilities of this new invention to the products they were producing. While in New York, he met with his old friend, Shido Yamada, who was living there. Yamada told Ibuka that Western Electric was offering to license the new transistor device, and Ibuka became confident that this new invention could be applied to consumer products, particularly to radios. He was of the opinion that, with transistors, radios could be small enough to be portable and could be sold in great quantities, especially in Third World countries where electric power was not available. He had already conceived the idea of these radios, which would operate on inexpensive flashlight batteries.

Kazuo Iwama, a young geophysicist who had joined the firm in June 1946, three weeks after its incorporation, had been in charge of tape recorder production. He was a confident, intelligent man from an aristocratic family, who had proven his ability in the years with Totsuko. Soon, he was caught up in the enthusiasm of Ibuka's vision for the future of transistors.

Ibuka advised him that he would be put in charge of the development of the transistor radio if they were successful in negotiating a license with Western Electric. Iwama was the third man of the trio which would be responsible for the birth of SONY, and the success of the transistor radio. However, it became the responsibility of Morita to negotiate a license from Western Electric.

In 1953, Morita made his first trip to New York, and with the help of Yamada, signed a provisional agreement, subject to the approval of MITI, the Japanese government's Ministry of International Trade and Industry. This was a calculated risk, since by law, before any firm could sign an agreement with a foreign company, approval had to be given by government bureaucrats. There were strict foreign currency restrictions in effect, and as the Western Electric agreement was subject to a royalty payment, Totsuko was acting without the necessary authority.

This was only one instance of the maverick reputation that Morita came to be known by in Japan, years before we met. It is doubtful whether his tiny company would have received permission had Morita applied in advance, because MITI would have considered Totsuko too small a firm to be given this authority. However, Ibuka, who was held in great respect because of his success in producing the first tape recorders in Japan, finally persuaded the government agency to issue the license.

Up to that time, the only licensed use of the transistor was for a hearing aid, manufactured by Zenith. Raytheon had obtained a license, and because it was a low-frequency transistor, they had impressed upon Zenith its adaptation for use in hearing aids. As a result, Zenith had been able to produce a much smaller three transistor unit then available at the time. Although the hearing aid was a financial success, the market was limited. At that time, it never occurred to Zenith to try to adapt the transistor to high frequency use, as required for portable radios.

However, at the same time that Totsuko, with Iwama in charge, was expending every effort to unravel the mystery of this adaptation, two engineers from Texas Instruments had conceived the same idea. They soon obtained a license from Western Electric, and in short order they were successful in producing the world's first transistor radio Regency. However, it was not of the quality that Ibuka and his team were striving to achieve.

Would SONY have been what they became if they had not seized the opportunity that came their way?

It was my good fortune to meet Akio Morita in 1955. Akio Morita was in his early thirties when we first met. I was struck first by the brightness of his eyes behind the glasses he wore. An energetic young man of about five feet, nine inches in height, he had dark hair parted in the middle, was fairly slight of build, spoke English but not very well at that time and he had an aristocratic air about him. Unlike his heroic counterparts who would also change the face of consumer products in the second half of the 20th century, such as the founder of the Honda Motor company, Soichiro Honda, who was the son of a blacksmith and who began his career as a bicycle repair-boy, Morita was educated and well-off.

It was in August 1955, that Ibuka's team perfected the first transistor adaptable to high frequency and suitable for radio manufacture. That October, after the first production run of the TR55, the news item appeared in the *Nippon Times* announcing the product, which would attract my attention on that fortunate second visit to Japan. With the benefit of hindsight, this proved to be the most providential happening in the history of General Distributors Ltd. It turned out to be very good for a very small Japanese company named Tokyo Tsushin Kogyo, soon to be changed to the name of "SONY". Totsuko's sales volume was a mere $2 million in 1955 when we first met, while General Distributor's sales were much greater.

Totsuko was stymied as how to market the radio because the retail market was controlled by well-known Japanese manufacturers such as Matsushita (known as Panasonic), Toshiba, Hitachi, NEC and others.

As an example Matsushita controlled up to twenty-five thousand small retailers. Not by owning them outright but by putting their manufactured products such as rice cookers, toasters, irons, and other products, in these stores on a consignment basis. The proviso was that these stores would not sell or buy any competitor products.

They would pay for these products only when they sold the items. Each month representatives of Matsushita would check their inventories. Only then would they be billed to pay for the merchandise sold.

Other manufacturers had similar arrangements so that the market was closed for a new small manufacturer such as Totsuko.

In the meantime other manufacturers would soon be producing transistor radios under their well-known brand names on the Japanese markets. Totsuko had a brief window of time to be first in the market with their radio but there was no way they could display or sell their product in large quantities.

When we became export customers of Totsuko and showed them the way to go was through export, it gave Morita the solution to their problem. As our orders grew in volume Morita decided that if in his words, "that far northern country of ice and snow" inhabited by Royal Canadian Mounted Police and with a small population, surely they could make headway in exporting to the United States.

It did not take long for Morita, sometimes against the advice of his superiors, to show that this was the direction for Totsuko in the future growth of the company. It was not long after the early success in the United States that Morita rose in the ranks from General Manager to the President of the company.

Masaru Ibuka the original founder of the company moved up to Chairman. He then handed over the reins for growth to Akio Morita as the President and Chief Executive Officer.

TOKYO TSUSHIN KOGYO, LTD.

351 KITASHINAGAWA-6, SHINAGAWA-KU
TOKYO JAPAN

Date: Nov.2, '55

To: General Distributors Ltd.
791 Notre Dame Avenue
Winnipeg, Canada

CABLE : TAPECORDER TOKYO
PHONE : 49-0166

No. E-89

Proforma Invoice

item	description	q'ty	unit price	amount
	Transistor Radio TR-55 (Set & Extra Antenna)	50	FOB Yokohama $27.00	$1,350.00

GDL
WINNIPEG
VIA VANCOUVER
MADE IN JAPAN
CASE #1

Shipment: November 18, 1955
Payment: standard L/C or Cheque
Packing: standard export packing

Tokyo Tsushin Kogyo, Ltd.

A. Morita
Managing Director

Totsuko's (later known as **SONY***) first invoice for export outside of Japan.*

Japanese Technology
Meets Canadian Salesmanship

Before leaving for Hawaii, where Irena was awaiting my return, I arranged a final meeting with Akio Morita. I had decided that the TR55, at $79.95 retail, was too expensive for resale and would not find a ready market. I had, however, decided that I would purchase fifty of these, to be used primarily for Christmas gifts, giving me a chance to test the market in the Winnipeg area. I was anxious to find out from Morita whether they would be producing another model which would be of better value. My experience with Japanese suppliers was that they were always forward looking and would produce products to suit the market demand in quality and price.

Morita agreed to ship the fifty TR55 radios, which went forward on November 2, 1955, from the port of Yokohama. *General Distributors thus became the first export customer of Tokyo Tsushin Kogyo Ltd.* The timing could not have been better for both of us. By purchasing the first shipment to be exported from Japan, we pioneered the import of transistor radios anywhere in the world. A most important fact came out in conversation with Morita: they were preparing a new model, named the TR72, which would be ready by the spring of 1956, and two sample models would be shipped to us as soon as available. The TR72 would be priced more reasonably, and Morita felt it would be more saleable in our market.

Although Morita and his associates were inventive geniuses, what they lacked was merchandising experience, which was, of course, our forte. This was not surprising; both Ibuka and Morita had tried to market a portable tape recorder in the States and had been singularly unsuccessful. Morita had even been to Toronto and had shown the tape recorder to the owners of a firm known as Sea Breeze. They were Japanese Nesei, and though they were impressed with the product, they assured Morita that a Japanese product by an unknown manufacturer could never be marketed in the face of such well-known brands as General Electric,

Zenith and RCA. They therefore turned down the opportunity of representing Totsuko in Canada.

I believe that one of my blessings is in being able to appraise people correctly. In the short time I had spent with Morita, I decided that I would take a soft approach, and not push for a contract at that time.

"Mr. Morita," I therefore said, "you do not know very much about me or my firm. We are a partnership of six brothers, two of whom are located in Winnipeg, and one each in the major Canadian cities of Vancouver, Calgary, Toronto and Montreal. I am the president and responsible for all contracts. At this time, all I want is your word of honour that, until you hear further from me, within a period no longer than six months, you give me the opportunity to test the new TR72 in the Canadian market. If you are happy, then you will consider our firm as your exclusive agent for Canada. If we are not successful, then I will release you from your promise. If we are successful, as I believe we will be, I will return to Japan and ask you to give us an exclusive contract."

When Morita agreed that this arrangement would be satisfactory, I thanked him warmly. In addition, I offered him some advice. I felt my experience in marketing Paper-Mate would be of extreme importance for Totsuko to follow, and made the following suggestions, along with an elaboration of the Triangle of Success:

1. If you wish to be successful in marketing, you must be scrupulous in your dealings with appointed distributors. Therefore, you must never sell your products to trading companies, such as the Zaibatsu, which does not understand the marketing of consumer products. A distributor must be able to appoint *his own* channels of distribution, especially in a country as huge as Canada

2. Never sacrifice quality for price. We do not want the cheapest price, but we *do* want the best quality at a reasonable cost.

3. In order to establish your product in a market, you must advertise extensively if you are to survive. The customer must be able to recognize your product by its brand name.

4. A good supply of parts for service replacements is necessary. No matter how good a product, service depots are of prime necessity, so that if a product fails because of factory defect or customer abuse, the customer will be able to have the product serviced within a reasonable period of time.

These were the main precepts that we both agreed upon in this meeting. It was left to me to set the retail price on the product and to establish the service and selling facilities. My parting words to Morita were, "I expect to make a reasonable profit on your product, and I expect you to do the same."

WE SEALED OUR AGREEMENT WITH A HANDSHAKE.

It was a few years later, through a close associate of both Ibuka and Morita's, that I learned the profound importance of this first meeting that I had with Tokyo Tsushin Kogyo. It was "Doc" Kagawa who told me of the discussions that went on in the inner circles of the company between two factions: those who believed that marketing efforts should be concentrated in Japan, with its captive population of over 100 million at that time, and those who believed their efforts should be directed toward export. General Distributors had dropped in, quite literally out of the blue, to support Morita's contention that **export** was the direction the company should go. At that time, Ibuka was the president and CEO, and the one who wielded the authority. But it was Morita, with his enthusiasm and tremendous vitality, who argued the export course as the one to take and who finally had his way. Time was to prove him right in his evaluation, and as the company grew and flourished, his importance and influence increased.

One further matter that I wished to attend to was moving our office in Tokyo to larger quarters. Frank Wertheimber made the arrangements, and before I left for Hawaii, the branch was established in the Tiger Building under the name of General Distributors (Tokyo) Ltd. The branch, with its staff of five, meant that we were now truly an international company.

When I returned to Hawaii, where Irena was awaiting my return, I decided to have a few days of rest on the beaches of Waikiki. While sunning on the beach, I decided that I would *not* proceed to Los Angeles to meet with Pat Frawley, as I had contemplated doing. Now that my arrangements in Japan had been made, it was necessary to concentrate on the immediate problem of the sale that Frawley had made to the Gillette Corporation of Boston, a fact I had been informed of by cablegram just before I left Tokyo. The question paramount in my mind was, *had Pat protected our exclusive distributorship arrangement in Canada,* as he had sworn to me, in making the sale to Gillette? I decided to phone him.

Frawley agreed that there was no point in having a meeting yet, since the lawyers were working on the finalization of the deal. He said that as soon as he had more information, he would contact me in Winnipeg.

I had taken some samples of the TR55 with me to show to my brothers when I returned to Winnipeg. The radio was small and easily transport-

Albert D. Cohen and Akio Morita, the famous handshake contract.

able. On checking the past year's statistics on sales of portable radios in Canada, we found that a total of only 24,000 had been sold in 1954. It was pointed out that even if this new product captured 50 per cent of the market, the dollar volume would not be of great importance.

Besides, who would pay $79 for an unknown brand manufactured in Japan, the argument went, when for $25 retail you could buy a General Electric, RCA or any number of well-known American portable tube radios? It did seem an almost impossible task to promote this product in our market.

It was then that the experience with Paper-Mate came to the rescue. I pointed out that people **will** pay for convenience. The Totsuko radio had convenience and performance as well: no more expensive "B" batteries or tubes to replace, thanks to the miracle invention of transistors, which provided months of use on ordinary flashlight batteries. I decided to wait and see what the new TR72 radio would look like, before a final decision was made. In the meantime, the sale of Paper-Mate to the Gillette Corporation required my immediate attention. After all, that company was the core of our business and our profits at that moment in our history.

Some Notes on Japanese
Business and Culture

My studies during many trips to Japan gave me some background on the trading houses that dominated the Japanese business world. These were the dominant companies, doing over 65 per cent of Japan's foreign trade. The Japanese referred to them as Sogo Shosha. Their combined revenue was equivalent to about 35 per cent of Japan's gross national product, and in 1954 they accounted for almost 80 per cent of Japan's exports world-wide.

In many cases, the Zaibatsu, as they are generally referred to in the West, financed many of the smaller manufacturers. Generally, the Zaibatsu group consisted of a bank, an insurance company, a shipping company and any facility connected with export, which could be handled through the group. It is evident that such a group would be considered a combine in the West, but for Japan it was a perfect method for penetrating world markets. Indeed, Japan itself has been called a Zaibatsu of Zaibatsus. It would have been impossible for the smaller companies of Japan to have made the progress that they did without the aid of the Zaibatsu.

After the Second World War, General MacArthur broke up the Zaibatsu, but by 1959 all the hundreds of companies had reassembled into eight big groups, called in order of size, Mitsubishi Corp., Mitsui & Co., C. Itoh, Sumitomo Corp., Nissho Iwai, Toyo Menka, Kanematsu Corp. and Nichimen Corp.

The Japanese are the greatest savers in the world, with up to 15 per cent of their income in savings accounts. So, through banks controlled by the Zaibatsu, a great source of funds was available to finance start-ups and developing companies. Some of these eventually grew to be giants in their field. Because there was no long-term financing available through an open market as in the western world, loans were advanced through the banks controlled by the Zaibatsu, on a short-term, roll-over basis. The manufacturing companies were thus at the mercy of the banks when it came to renewing their loans. If the company borrowing the money had good prospects, the Zaibatsu took an equity position and eventually controlled the company. If the company did not prosper, the bank withdrew its support and the company failed. That is why, even today, there are a great number of bankruptcies in Japan. The unsentimental Japanese do not believe in propping up failing companies, which number in the thousands every year. As I pen these words today, in 2002, the Japanese government, after the collapse of the Nikkei stock market, find it difficult to take the strong stand necessary with the Japanese banks to help improve the shaky economy.

One other important lesson I learned was through the many contacts I made with US importers, who usually congregated each evening in the famous Imperial Hotel bar. The Americans tended to do business with the Japanese as they would with their own counterparts in the States. They wanted instant decisions. This upset the managers of the firms with whom they were doing business. The Americans did not seem to understand the Japanese psyche, which allows decisions to be made by consensus, and not by individuals.

When a buyer who had imported an item found that it sold well in his market, he would decide that he could increase his repeat order substantially, and therefore a trip to the Orient was justified. He would then wish to negotiate a lower price on the item he was buying.

The intake of breath by the manager or owner of the business with whom he was negotiating was usually mistaken as an involuntary surprise at the size of the order he was proposing. He did not realize that going through the mind of the individual was the thought:

> How do I tell him that the order is too large for my modest factory? If I have the time, perhaps I can get some of my competitors to help me fill this order. But my foreign friend wants a reduction in price, and he is pretty adamant about that. I cannot insult this good customer of mine by saying I cannot oblige him, so I will agree to a price reduction. However, I will have to remove some of the quality where it will not be noticed, so that I can oblige my customer by giving him the discount he requested. This way, he will not lose face, and I will still make a profit.

The buyer would return to New York or Chicago and justify his trip by the lower price he obtained. The merchandise would arrive on schedule. Because of the success of previous shipments, the items would be readily sold. Soon, the returns would start, because of the reduced quality in the items. The purchaser would see the "Made in Japan" markings and blame the manufacturer and the country of origin.

The fault, then, lay with the manufacturer who did not understand foreign markets. The importer, of course, was also to blame for negotiating on price alone. He was looking for short-term profits, instead of building a reputation for quality in his products and going after long-term gains and relationships.

In most cases, the small manufacturer who wanted to export some of his production had no knowledge of how to accomplish this. That is when the Zaibatsu, who in most cases controlled the manufacturer, came into the picture. The Zaibatsu would make the contact in various countries for the sale of the manufacturer's products, without any knowledge of whether the agent in the country was properly situated geographically for the product. The Zaibatsu could not control after-sales or service. Consequently, you might find an exclusive contract signed in Regina for Canada-wide distribution, even though the firm would have no sales organization in the rest of Canada. This method of distribution also worked to the great disadvantage of the Japanese manufacturers, who were trying to establish a reputation for quality products in countries around the world.

On our return to Tokyo, I had by this time a chance to gain a better understanding of how to do business in Japan. I recognized that this country could be an excellent source of merchandise. The Brotman contact was a very important one. It seemed that the staff he had assembled had knowledge of the source of supply for almost any item I would be interested in bringing to Canada.

One thing I put into place immediately was that, before any manufacturer could draw payment on our letter of credit, they would have to obtain a certificate of inspection. Frank Wertheimber was to spot-inspect any shipments destined for us, and if there was any defect, it could be caught at the source. Although I found the Japanese suppliers in subsequent years very trustworthy and willing to adjust for any deficiencies, the cost of returning defective merchandise and claiming rebate of duties and taxes was exorbitant, time-consuming and inconvenient. It was much more satisfactory to have the inspection done before leaving Japan. Furthermore, knowing the merchandise would be inspected before they could draw against our letter of credit ensured that more attention was paid to shipments consigned to us. This did help, because the better quality of our imports began to be recognized by the customers of General Distributors.

Bushido – The Soul of Japan

On one of my many trips to Japan, after fifty, I stopped counting, a good friend whom I had known for many years presented me with a book. In the typical Japanese way it was wrapped in a beautiful rice paper, tied with a bright red ribbon. On opening the present I saw it was a book entitled *Bushido – The Soul of Japan* by Inanzo Nitobe A.M. PhD. It was published by Charles E. Tuttle Company, Rutland, Vermont and Tokyo, Japan.

I will refer to a number of incidents in Bushido. I believe this will give the reader a better understanding of the Japanese, their differences in their approach to the many every day contacts with the Western world.

The definition of Bushido is that it is the unwritten code of laws governing the lives and conduct of the nobles of Japan, equivalent in its day to in many ways European chivalry of the middle ages, and their retainers known as the samurai.

For a better understanding of Bushido, which gives some insight to the Japanese character, I will relate some incidents illustrated by the author Nitobe. His book was written and first published in 1905. Its purpose was an attempt to illustrate to foreigners the comparison between Japanese versus Western ways.

On Politeness

"In America, when you make a gift, you sing its praises to the recipient; in Japan we deprecate or slander it. The underlying idea is, "This is a nice gift, if it were not nice, I would not dare to give it to you; for it will be an insult to give you anything but what is nice."

In contrast to this, the Japanese logic runs: "You are a nice person, and no gift is nice enough for you. You will not accept anything I can lay at your feet except as a token of my good will; so accept this, not for its intrinsic value, but as a token. It will be an insult to your worth to call the best gift good enough for you."

"Place the two ideas side by side, and we see that the ultimate idea is one and the same."

Position of a Woman

"To me it seems that our idea of marital union goes in some ways further than the so-called Christian. "Man and woman shall be one flesh." The individualism of the Anglo-Saxon cannot let go of the idea that husband and wife are two persons; hence, when they disagree, their separate rights are recognized, and when they agree, they exhaust their vocabulary in all sorts of silly pet names and nonsensical blandishments.

It sounds highly irrational to our ears, when a husband or wife speaks to a third party of his or her other half, better or worse, as being lovely, bright, kind and what not. Is it good taste to speak of one's self as "my bright self," "my lovely disposition," and so forth?

The Japanese think praising one's own wife is praising a part of one's own self, and self-praise is regarded, to say the least, as bad taste among us, and I hope, among Christian nations too! I have diverged at some length because the polite debasement of one's consort was a usage most in vogue among the samurai."

The Japanese Love of the Cherry Blossom - Influence of Bushido

> *"Isles of blest Japan!*
>
> *Should your Yamato spirit*
>
> *Strangers seek to scan,*
>
> *Say-scenting morn's sunlit air,*
>
> *Blows the cherry wild and air!"*

"Yes, the sakura has for ages been the favourite of our people and the emblem of our character. Mark particularly the terms of definition which the poet uses, the words *the wild cherry flower scenting the morning sun.*

The Yamato spirit is not a tame, tender plant, but a wild-in sense of natural growth; it is indigenous to the soil; its accidental qualities it may share with the flowers of other lands, but in its essence it remains the original, spontaneous outgrowth of our clime. But its nativity is not its sole claim to our affection. The refinement and grace of its beauty appeal to our aesthetic sense as no other flower can."

Our Thoughts on the Rose

"We cannot share the admiration of the Europeans for their roses, which lack the simplicity of our flower. Then too, the thorns that are hidden beneath the sweetness of the rose, the tenacity with which she clings to life, as though loth or afraid to die rather than drop untimely, preferring to rot on her stem; her showy colours and heavy odors all these are traits so unlike the cherry blossom, which carries no dagger or poison under its beauty, which is ever ready to depart life at the call of nature, whose colours are never gorgeous, and whose light fragrance never palls. Beauty of colour and of form is limited in its showing; it is a fixed quality of existence, whereas fragrance is volatile, ethereal as the breathing of life. So in all religious ceremonies frankincense and myrrh play a prominent part. There is something spirituelle in redolence.

When the delicious perfume of the sakura quickens the morning air, as the sun in its course rises to illumine first the isles of the Far East, few sensations are more serenely exhilarating than to inhale, as it were, the very breath of beauteous day.

When the Creator Himself is pictured as making new resolutions in His heart upon smelling a sweet savour (Gen. Viii.21), is it any wonder that the sweet smelling season of the cherry blossom should call forth the whole nation from their little habitations? Blame them not, if for a time their limbs forget their toil and moil and their hearts their pangs and sorrows. Their brief pleasure ended, they return to their daily task with new strength and new resolutions."

"THUS IN WAYS MORE THAN ONE IS THE SAKURA THE
FLOWER OF THE NATION."

Is Bushido Still Alive on Religion?

"One cause of the failure of mission work is that most of the missionaries are entirely ignorant of our history. "What do we care for heathen records?" some say and consequently estrange their religion from the habits of thought we and our forefathers have been accustomed to for centuries past. Mocking a nation's history? As though the career of any people even of the lowest African savages possessing no record were not a page in the general history of mankind, written by the hand of God Himself. The very lost races are a palimpsest to be deciphered by a seeing-eye. To a philosophic and pious mind the races themselves are marks of Divine chirography clearly traced in black and white as on their skin; and if this simile holds good, the yellow race forms a precious page inscribed in hieroglyphics of gold!"

Suicide and Redress

An interesting translation by the author Mitford in his Tales of Old Japan from a rare Japanese manuscript describes an execution of an eyewitness to a *seppuku* better known in the western world as hara-kiri which means self-immolation by disembowelment.

"We, seven foreign representatives, were invited to follow the Japanese witnesses into the *hondo* or main hall of the temple, where the ceremony was to be performed. It was an imposing scene. A large hall with a high roof supported by dark pillars of wood. From the ceiling hung a profusion of those huge gilt lamps and ornaments peculiar to Buddhist temples. In front of the high altar, where the floor, covered with beautiful white mats, is raised some three or four inches from the ground, was laid a rug of scarlet felt. Tall candles placed at regular intervals gave out a dim mysterious light, just sufficient to let all the proceedings be seen. The seven Japanese took their places on the left of the raised floor, the seven foreigners on the right. No other person was present."

"After the interval of a few minutes of anxious suspense, Taki Zenzaburo, a stalwart man thirty-two years of age, with a noble air, walked into the hall attired in his dress of ceremony, with the peculiar hempen-cloth wings which are worn on great occasions. He was accompanied by a *kaishaku* and three officers, who wore the *jimbaori* or war surcoat with gold tissue facings. The word Kaishaku, it should be observed, is one to which our word executioner is no equivalent term. The office is that of a gentleman; in many cases it is performed by a kinsman or friend of the condemned, and the relation between them is rather that of principal and second than that of victim and executioner. In this instance, the kaishaku was a pupil of Taki Zenzaburo, and was selected by friends of the latter from among their own number for his skill in swordsmanship."

"With the kaishaku on his left hand, Taki Zenzaburo advanced slowly toward the Japanese witnesses, and the two bowed before them, then drawing near to the foreigners they saluted us in the same way, perhaps even more deference; in each case the salutation was ceremoniously returned. Slowly and with great dignity the condemned man mounted on to the raised floor, prostrated himself before the high altar twice, and seated himself on the felt carpet with his back to the high altar, the kaishaku crouching on his left-hand side. One of the three attendant officers then came forward, bearing a stand of the kind used in the temple for offerings, on which, wrapped in paper, lay the *wakizashi,* the short sword or dirk of the Japanese, nine inches and a half in length, with a point and an edge as sharp as a razor's. This he handed, prostrating himself, to the condemned man, who received it reverently raising it to his head with both hands, and placed it in front of himself."

"After another profound obeisance, Taki Zenzaburo, in a voice which betrayed just so much emotion and hesitation as might be expected from a man who is making a painful confession, but with no sign of either in his face or manner, spoke as follows:

I, and I alone, unwarrantably gave the order to fire on the foreigners at Kobe, and again as they tried to escape. For this crime I disembowel myself, and I beg you who are present to do me the honour of witnessing the act."

"Bowing once more, the speaker allowed his upper garments to slip down to his girdle, and remained naked to the waist. Carefully, according to custom, he tucked his sleeves under his knees to prevent himself from falling backward; for a noble Japanese gentleman should die falling forwards. Deliberately, with a steady hand he took the dirk that lay before him; he looked at it wistfully, almost affectionately; for a moment he seemed to collect his thoughts for the last time, and then stabbing himself deeply below the waist in the left-hand side, he drew the dirk slowly across to his right side, and turning it in the wound, gave a slight cut upwards. During this sickeningly painful operation he never moved a muscle of his face. When he drew out the dirk, he leaned forward and stretched out his neck; an expression of pain for the first time crossed his face, but he uttered no sound. At that moment the kaishaku, who, still crouching by his side, had been keenly watching his every movement, sprang to his feet, poised his sword for a second in the air; there was a flash, a heavy, ugly thud, a crashing fall; with one blow, the head had been severed from the body."

"A dead silence followed, broken only by the hideous noise of the blood throbbing out of the insert heap before us, which but a moment before had been a brave and chivalrous man. It was horrible."

"The kaishaku made a low bow, wiped his sword with a piece of paper which he had ready for the purpose, and retired from the raised floor; and the stained dirk was solemnly borne away, a bloody proof of the execution."

"The two representatives of the Mikado then left their places, and crossing over to where the foreign witnesses sat, called to us to witness that the sentence of death upon Taki Zenzaburo had been faithfully carried out. The ceremony being at an end, we left the temple."

Although this book by Inazo Nitobe was written in 1905 describing Bushido The Soul of Japan it perhaps gives some insight even today at the end of the last century of how different the Japanese approach to life and manners is to the Western culture, religion and psyche.

In my experiences with the Japanese there can be so much misunderstanding in language particularly. In a social, business or political meeting in discussions the Japanese will do everything to avoid a confrontation. They will seldom give a direct refusal to a proposal. "Yes" means we will consider your request upon consultation whereas to a Westerner it means an affirmative answer. "Maybe" to a Westerner means we will consider it while to a Japanese it is a polite refusal. It is very seldom you have a definite "no".

In my experience in negotiations it is not to demand a definite answer to a request. It is best to put the onus on the person after pointing out the reason for the request and how it will benefit both parties. A confrontation is best to be avoided at all times.

This explanation of the difference in cultures is perhaps best explained by an article that appeared in the Okura News under the heading "Japanology" by Makio Matsusaka.

"At the same time, there was a very distinct class system called *shi-no-ko-sho*. *Shi* were the samurai class; *no* the farmers; *ko* the craftsmen and artisans and *sho* the merchants and traders. Although the samurai were the highest rank in this social order, they had little money. The merchant, on the other hand, had the most money of these four classes.

Whenever a merchant met a samurai, he had to make a very low kowtow to the samurai. If a merchant should meet a samurai on the street who showed a piece of cloth to him, saying, "this cloth is blue, it is very expensive because it is blue and you should buy it from me for a very high price because it is blue," even though the cloth might be almost white, the merchant, even though he knows it is almost white and that he should pay a much lower price because it is not top quality, cannot say "No, Mr. Samurai, it is not blue; it's almost all white."

He cannot because by doing so he could very easily lose his head for arguing with a person of a higher rank, a samurai. Instead, what he would say is, "Yes, Mr. Samurai, yes, yes, but to my eyes, which are probably not as good as yours, the blue color is not strong enough to give a higher price."

The samurai could not fight the merchant because he hadn't said "no," he had not disagreed with the samurai, he had only said that to his eyes, in his opinion, it looked less blue. That's all. The samurai now must negotiate the price, which he does because the merchant has the money that the samurai needs. Ultimately, he will accept the price the merchant offers. This is a typical example of negotiating in the Tokugawa era. Naturally no one wants to be killed simply for saying "no" so the people developed the "yes, but ..." technique to temporize before getting to the negotiation point.

Even today, in meetings, for example with the company president, everybody tries to know what the president thinks, to know the direction of his thinking. And everyone tries to ride on the president's opinion, not to be against his opinion, but to give additional or significant modification so that the president will not become disturbed or annoyed. Therefore, again no one will say "no" to the president's opinion, but everybody will say, "Yes, yes, yes, that's good, that's good, but ..."

I have an opinion about this and that is that there is no "no" but instead there is "yes, but ..." and this knowledge of how to live well, confronted with the problem of living in a small country with a large population, is going to continue for many, many years in Japan.

Perhaps the narrative in the episode related in "Suicide and Redress" will shock a westerner. However, even to this day, the senior officer in a corporation or a government senior official feels honour bound to atone for his mistakes or misconduct. Occasionally suicides have been committed because of failure in which the individual felt responsible. Sometimes it was by throwing themselves in front of a train and others who committed the act did so by jumping into the volcano on Mount Fuji, Japan's sacred mountain.

I personally believe that the Japanese example is more honourable than the episodes of the failure in businesses in the western world. The chief executives who have been responsible for these massive failures and walked away with many tens of millions of dollars as a reward for their failures cannot be sleeping well at night.

Okumura Negotiation by Consensus

Being aware of the fact that decisions are not made by individuals even by the president but by consultation with a group of the senior executives, I will relate an incident of why Akio Morita was looked upon as a maverick and was a man who made decisions on the basis of his own convictions. Our joint venture was formed in 1975. Mr. Morita at the time asked if Mr. Okumura could represent the SONY Tokyo interests in our joint venture. Of course I agreed and Okumura, better known as "Okie", became very much a part of the future Japanese which were integrating into the SONY of Canada operation.

On an occasion where the subject of decisions by consultations were made I will relate this incident. At our meeting I turned to Okumura and said, "Okie, from the story of Bushido I know that decisions are made through consultation. Regarding Gendis and SONY Tokyo, Mr. Morita made the decision on his own."

Okumura explained, "Oh, no, Mr. Cohen, I was one of a group of four that were asked to consult with regard to the decision and we had a deep discussion on the subject."

I said, "Then, Okie, obviously you all agreed with Mr. Morita's decision to form our joint venture." I said this proudly as it was well-known that we were the only company in the world with which SONY had agreed to a joint venture, particularly, where we had 51% and SONY Tokyo owned 49%.

I was rather surprised by the reply of Okumura. He said, "No, Mr. Cohen, we did not agree that a joint venture should be formed with General Distributors Limited. All three of us disagreed as SONY had always taken over full ownership in the countries where they were established."

I said, "Well then was this decision made by Mr. Morita on his own because of his ownership?"

I was rather amused by Okumura's reply when he said, "Yes. We were the majority that disagreed."

Mr. Morita's reply was, "I thank you for your opinion, but I am going to go ahead with this joint venture because in my judgement this is the right thing to do."

Okumura then ended the conversation saying, "Well, it was not so bad because we won our decision but only lost by one vote."

Albert D. Cohen.

On the Humorous Side

In the Chinese language, because they're alphabet does not contain the letter "R", where it occurs in conversation with an Oriental of the Chinese culture they pronounce such words as "bring" as "bling".

In Japanese who have adapted the KANJI variation of the English language, because their alphabet does not contain the letter "L", pronounce the letter as "R". As an example, "baseball" becomes "basebarru". This brings me to relate this episode.

When our SONY of Canada Ltd. sales manager, a division of Gendis Inc. was calling on a university, which shall remain nameless, the professor who was responsible in recommending the brand of electronic recording equipment for their medical department was a Japanese, well respected for his knowledge and teaching abilities. Almost all the electronics used at the university were of the SONY brand.

Our representative, while demonstrating the SONY equipment, which was a formality as the university had exclusively established SONY as their preferred equipment. It was necessary however for the professor to put his stamp of approval on the new product being offered.

In the course of conversation, the salesman pulled out a package of Du Maurier cigarettes and offered one to the professor, who politely refused. Arthur then flicked his Bic, as the expression goes, and proceeded to light his cigarette, inhaling deeply and then exhaling with satisfaction. Whereupon the professor said to Arthur, "Prease Mr. Arthur, can I have your rungs".

Arthur, mystified said, "My what? I'm sorry, I don't understand." "I said, your rungs, come with me and I wirr show you what I mean". He then proceeded to walk through a hall leading to his laboratory, Arthur following in his footsteps.

As they entered the laboratory, the professor pointed to a row of lungs taken from cadavers all of which had been placed on display on one of the walls of the laboratory. The lungs were in various tones of yellow discoloration in obvious deterioration forms of cancer.

"You see Mr. Arthur, I rike you very much. You serr me good SONY products which I need to continue my research and teaching for my students", he said and then continued, "but if you continue to smoke, your rungs wirr be on dispray in my raboratory in not to rong a time. That is why I asked if I courd have your rungs," he concluded.

Since that day Arthur has not lit a cigarette and quit smoking cold turkey as the saying goes. It is now common practice that if anyone lights a cigarette in my presence I ask the question, "Prease, can I have your rungs?"

A further humorous story dealing with this same professor concerns a luncheon date where he was to visit my office together with an attractive blonde assistant professor who acted as his girl Friday. She arranged his various appointments, lectures and acted as his general secretary.

On the appointed day, my secretary told me that the professor was calling and wished to speak with me regarding our luncheon. Evidently, some university unforeseen business was going to interfere with our luncheon date.

Imagine my surprise on taking his call when he said, "Mr. Cohen, so sorry but must cancer our appointment because I have important erection and must go with my secretary."

At first, I was flabbergasted at the frankness of his statement, but I immediately surmised that there must be a language interpretation that was not being declared. Cautiously, I asked "When did this happen?" "Oh", the professor replied, "did not happen yet, but I must be there with Ann, as we must vote for our facurty budget so we can have money to buy SONY equipment for the next term. So sorry but this is very important erection, so maybe we can have runch another day".

Not knowing the professor's sexual personal life I was happy for the sake of SONY that he was going to be at the election with Ann to pass on the budget for the next year's electronic requirements.

To finish this chapter, I will relate two anecdotes well known in Japanese folklore.

A Japanese beggar frequented a fish house where the most succulent odors were wafted through the door. Two merchants were contemplating a dish of *fugu,* one of the most tasty but dangerous fish to eat. It contains a highly poisonous liver which if not removed by the cook who has to be an expert in his craft could mean instantaneous death.

One of the merchants turned to the other and said, "Let us give a portion of this dish to the beggar outside before we partake of our feast."

"Good idea," his companion said, and that was done. After an interlude they looked out and saw that the beggar was healthy and well.

"Good," they said and proceeded to devour their food.

After a while the beggar came through the door. He said, "I see good sirs you enjoyed your dinner and you seem to be well and healthy. Now, I can enjoy the fugu fish you so kindly gave me."

Another anecdote concerns a restaurant whose tempting aromas were wafted out on the street to lure the passer-bys in to dine.

To the consternation of the owner, the town's wealthy but miserly man would walk up and down past his restaurant but never came in to dine or spend any money.

Frustrated he confronted this individual and said, "From now on, I am going to charge you for walking by my restaurant, smelling my food but never spending any money with me."

The next day as the miser walked by he was confronted by the owner, who demanded payment. The miser jangled the silver in his pocket and said, "I am only smelling your food so I will repay you by letting you hear the sound of my silver ringing in my pocket where the money will stay."

Our First Years with the Future SONY Corp.

Early in 1956, the long awaited samples of the new TR72 arrived by air in Winnipeg from Japan.

As I was making a trip to Ottawa, I used the opportunity to arrange an appointment to see David Sim, the Deputy Minister of National Revenue. Through my past experience, I had found that if we were contemplating the import of a new product, and if there were prospects of large volume, it was wise to touch base with the government. Once a product made an impact in the marketplace, it did not take long for competitors to lodge protests with Ottawa, complaining "these imports are taking away jobs from Canadians!" It was an old tradition for Canadian manufacturers in eastern Canada, instead of being innovators and trying to compete, to complain to Ottawa to enlist legislation, either barring an import entirely, or raising tariffs to such an extent that the imports could not compete fairly. This went back to the time of John A. Macdonald, the first Prime Minister of Canada, who enacted tariff legislation to protect eastern manufacturers. This has been remedied with the Free Trade deal with the U.S.A. and Mexico. The world in general is much more open in trade so ultimately, the public benefits without the punitive tariffs of the earlier years.

Fortunately, when I showed David Sim the TR55 and demonstrated its tone and power, all from four low-cost penlight batteries, he was suitably impressed. I predicted that in a few years, the transistor radio would be one of our largest import items, and asked for his blessing to import the radios, because I did not want to spend the time and effort to develop the sale, and then find that Ottawa would put roadblocks in the way of importation.

I pointed out that we had invested large sums of money in buildings in Winnipeg and Vancouver. At that time, we had many employees across Canada. I noted that the taxes that were assessed in the form of duties, sales and excise against imports helped government revenue. Importers had contributed to the Canadian economy. David Sim reassured me, "Albert, your arguments are valid. Don't worry about increasing your imports from Japan."

The total trade between Canada and Japan during 1954, the year before I met Akio Morita, was a mere $100 million. Canadian imports from Japan totaled only $20 million, while our exports to Japan were $80 million, an imbalance of four to one. Ottawa was receiving quite a bit of pressure because of this, and Canada was interested in improving trade with Japan. Some of the so-called Canadian radios were assembled in Canada, from import components, but most were imported from the US.

If we could increase our imports from Japan it would help adjust our imbalance of trade with that country.

My remarks to David Sim about the future of radio and electronic imports from Japan proved to be true. In the next few years, millions of radios and other electronic products poured into Canada. Fortunately for General Distributors, SONY was the pioneer, and we participated in this new era when trade turned to Asia.

When the three samples of the TR72 arrived by air, I was immediately impressed by this second transistor radio manufactured by Totsuko under the SONY brand. The price quoted, $24 FOB factory, meant that it would land in Canada for about $38, all duties, taxes and transportation included.

I realized that I would have to give the sales of this radio my personal attention, as it would require a convincing story as to why the TR72 should command a premium price over the better-known brand names on the market. I knew, as I've noted before, that people would pay for convenience. This model was a mantel type, and because of the wooden case and the larger speaker, it produced better sound than many of the giant cabinet radios that were standard furniture in most North American living rooms of the day.

I was certain that because of its portability, there would be a good market for this radio. After making a number of calls on some of our better accounts, I found that the resistance was greater than I had expected. No one seemed to be interested in paying a premium price for an unknown radio. They all seemed to be impressed with the performance, but not ready to make a commitment.

Finally, I decided to call on the buyer of the T. Eaton Co. Ltd. in Winnipeg. In the middle fifties, they were the leading department store chain in Canada, especially in Winnipeg, where they dominated the retail trade.

Since Eaton's enjoyed about 25 per cent of the total retail sales in the city at the time, their acceptance of a new product was equal to an endorsement. Because other merchants watched Eaton's advertising very closely, acceptance by Eaton's very often led to the product's success with other customers who watched them closely. I telephoned and made an appointment with Mr. Alf Wallis, the electrical department buyer.

"What are you selling?" he asked, with interest.

"What I have for you is just as revolutionary an item in radios as the Paper-Mate pens our company sold to your stationery department buyer, Sid Florence!" I exclaimed with enthusiasm. This piqued his interest, and an appointment was arranged.

The next day, I met Alf Wallis for the first time. Even though he was the manager of the department, as well as the buyer, he had no knowledge of the new transistor technology. He would have dismissed the product at once, if he had not been amazed by how, when I turned on the TR72, we had immediate good reception in his office. I opened the back of the radio, showed him that it operated on transistors and the power of three ordinary flashlight batteries. I tried as best as I could to explain the technology behind this new invention.

Although Wallis was interested, he held back. "I can't place an order for a new product such as this, unless it's checked out by Eaton's research department in Toronto," he informed me, "and it must be cleared, as to the reliability of claims made."

"How is this procedure arranged?" I queried.

"The buyers for Eaton's stores across Canada meet twice a year, spring and fall," he explained. "At that time, orders are placed, so that arrangements can be made with suppliers to buy on a quantity basis for all stores, in order to get maximum discounts. At the same time, new products are presented and considered by all the buyers, as a committee, for approval."

I persuaded Alf Wallis to take a sample with him the following week, as he was leaving for the spring trip to Toronto. Would he arrange to have the TR72 put through their testing laboratory? Even if the radio was turned down by their buyers, at least I would have their expert opinion to either confirm or deny the quality I claimed for the TR72.

Wallis agreed, and I left the sample with him.

It was about two weeks later that I received a call from him. He had just returned from Toronto and asked me to come to his office as he had the report for me. That afternoon, Wallis explained what had transpired on his trip to the head office.

When he boarded the train in Winnipeg, he decided to take the TR72 with him. Like most Canadians, Wallis enjoyed listening to the hockey broadcasts on Saturday evenings, the still-famous and popular "Hockey Night in Canada." At that time there were only six teams in the National Hockey League. The intense rivalry between the two Canadian teams, the Montreal Canadiens and the Toronto Maple Leafs, was further heightened by the staccato delivery of Foster Hewitt, who broadcasted the play-by-play action of the games.

On this Saturday night, there was particular interest in the game being played. It was the last one of the semi-finals between Toronto and Detroit, to decide who would be opposing the winners of the New York Rangers - Montreal Canadiens series.

After Wallis got settled for the long trip to Toronto, he noticed that a number of people had portable radios, and were tuned in to the game. He then decided to turn on the TR72, and was not surprised when the broadcast came in loud and clear. Soon, he became engrossed in the play-by-play action.

After about an hour, when the train entered the Lake of the Woods area, the beginning of the rocky Precambrian Shield where the mineral riches of Canada are primarily located, Wallis became conscious that he was gradually being surrounded by the passengers in his coach. As he looked around, he became aware that all the other portable radios had ceased functioning once the train had entered the rock-cuts of the shield. *The TR72 was still bringing in the signal, loud and clear!* Not only did everyone want to hear the final outcome of the game, but many wanted to know where they could buy this radio that out-performed their own portables.

This convinced Wallis, more than anything, that there was a massive potential market for this new product. The first thing he did, the Monday morning of the Eaton's meeting, was to have the TR72 tested in their laboratory. Three days later, he received the test report, which was superbly affirmative in all directions. If we at General Distributors were the first export customer in the world for what would be SONY radios, then Eaton's was the first retailer to buy SONY anywhere outside Japan.

The order that Alf Wallis placed was for 188 TR72s. On this basis, I immediately wrote to Totsuko and ordered 2,000 of the TR72 radios. I knew that we would be successful in selling the balance to other retailers, once it became known that Eaton's was selling this radio. Because the name SONY was unknown, I asked for the TR72 to be branded as "Gendis

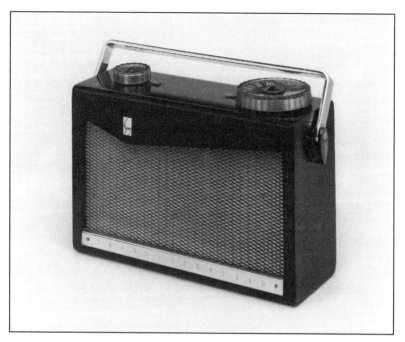

SONY transistor radio, model TR72.

SONY." In my letter to Akio Morita, I pointed out that the Gendis brand was known and trusted in Canada, and that we had branded our quality imports such as watches, diamonds and other fine items, with this name. Therefore, I felt that this Japanese made radio could be introduced by riding piggy-back under our name. For the first two years, all imports of SONY products to Canada carried the name of Gendis SONY, the only time and place this was done in the history of that remarkable Japanese firm. It was only after SONY started its phenomenal and sensational growth that we voluntarily dropped the Gendis portion of the name and emphasized, in advertising, the brand name SONY.

That year, we imported a total of 10,000 radios, generating an excellent volume of sales. This was still a relatively small part of our total business, but I was convinced that the potential of this new product would be great. In view of this, a hefty portion of our first revenue was spent on advertising, point of sale material, catalogue sheets, and more. The true potential was in the *future* growth of the new products that would follow.

As I had predicted when I visited David Sim in Ottawa, the sale of transistor radios really started to develop in 1958. That year, SONY introduced the TR63, a radio that would fit in a shirt pocket. True, it was slightly larger than that, but SONY had some shirts made with slightly larger pockets, so that when the salesmen were demonstrating this radio, it could easily fit! This radio was an overnight success, and helped increase our sales to 30,000 radios, a considerable rise over the previous year.

It was time to start thinking of a contract between SONY and General Distributors. Because of the trust and splendid cooperation between our two companies, I was not too concerned. On my visits to Tokyo, I usually dealt with Akio Morita himself, as we had developed a close friendship. I was often invited to his home in Tokyo and spent many pleasant evenings in the company of his charming wife, Yoshiko. Their two sons, Hideo and Masao, and the youngest child Naoko, a lovely young girl were usually present. He must have considered me a good friend, since his wife actually cooked the meals, handing the food through an open slot from the kitchen, after which she would come and join us in their dining room. In those early years, the Morita's lived in a very modest home.

Morita had become an ardent golfer, and on weekends he usually arranged a foursome. Like all things that interested him, he had scientifically analyzed his swing, and it was not too long before he was playing in the low nineties. Probably one of his greatest satisfactions was in winning chocolate bars and golf balls, the stakes we usually played for. Often, Mr. Ibuka joined us on these weekends. I usually brought my golf shoes with me, as my size is a 13A. I knew that if I forgot to bring them, it would be difficult to get that size in those days in Tokyo.

Akio Morita Visits Winnipeg 1957

At this time, General Distributors Ltd. was headquartered at 791 Notre Dame Avenue in Winnipeg, an office space of about 3,500 square feet, and 9,000 square feet of warehouse. Company sales were growing rapidly, and we had outgrown our facilities, but we hesitated to expand, because of the expense of moving to larger quarters. One day, I received word that Akio Morita, together with "Doc" Kagawa and two other executives, were coming to visit us in Winnipeg. I emphasized to our directors that this would be a very important visit and that we should impress them with our facilities and our efforts to expand and develop the sales of SONY in Canada.

The SONY group arrived from Tokyo on schedule. Morita advised me that they were enroute to Chicago to attend the electronics show in that city. Because of our increasing sales, they had decided to come to Winnipeg first. He then showed me two models of new radios that they were planning to introduce early in 1958, the TR608 and the TR75.

The TR608 was a six-transistor radio, while the TR75 was a seven-transistor. At that time, radios were sold based on the number of transistors they incorporated in their design. They were both attractively cased in various colours of plastic. After due consideration, we established that the TR608 would retail at $49.95, while the TR75 could sell for the price of $59.95. I advised Morita that I would place an order with him for 1,000 of each model. To my surprise, he asked me to increase this order to *5,000* of each. He assured me that from all statistics and studies they had made in Tokyo, the demand for transistor radios was due for a tremendous upsurge.

I asked to adjourn our meeting for an hour, so that I could consult with my brothers. A purchase of 10,000 radios at that time represented an investment that could heavily strain our financial resources. At $14 each, plus duties and other costs to land would exceed over $200,000, which was a large amount to have tied up in inventory at that time.

To say that I had unanimity in our discussion would be an exaggeration, but having full confidence in Morita, I was able to convince my partners to confirm this order. After resuming our meeting, we confirmed to Morita an order totaling 10,000 radios. At the same time, I brought up the subject of a contract between our two companies. It was arranged that we would meet in Chicago for a preliminary discussion later that week.

The SONY group was staying at the Conrad Hilton Hotel in Chicago, so I arranged a reservation there. After attending the electronics show, we met in the main dining room. During dinner and in conversation, Morita assured me that SONY was happy with our representation in Canada. He suggested that a five-year contract be concluded with "Albert D. Cohen," instead of General Distributors Ltd. He said that he knew me, but not the rest of the brothers, and all our deals had been negotiated between the two of us.

At first I felt flattered, but on reflection I realized that this was the way the automobile companies arranged franchises in their various territories. If they wished to terminate an agency, it was much simpler to deal with an individual, rather than a company. Furthermore, if an agent died, then the contract died with the individual. This gave the manufacturer the option to either renew a deal with the heirs, or terminate an unproductive arrangement. All this passed through my mind, and I very carefully chose my words to Morita.

"Akio, my five brothers are equal partners in our operation. For that reason, I *cannot* let myself be put in a position where *I* would have control of this agency." Then, I added another concern: "As we require financing from our bankers, the only thing they would recognize for security was a contract with the company."

After some discussion in Japanese with his associates, Morita turned to me and said that he understood the points I was making. We then arranged that we would meet the following month in Tokyo to finalize our agreement.

To show the perception of Akio Morita and his ability to judge the market, it should be noted that 1958 proved to be the watershed year of the transistor radio market. The breakthrough in sales that he had predicted happened beyond wildest expectations. SONY had produced an eight transistor radio of excellent quality, the TR84 and a number of other innovations, including the first transistorized short-wave AM/FM radio. Our sales in 1958 reached 80,000 SONY radios, and by 1959 we exceeded 100,000.

Our advertising, which featured the new SONY name, was increased proportionately as sales grew, and was extended to include magazines, weeklies, newspapers, radio and television. I told everyone that every dollar spent in advertising SONY was an investment in the future; after all, our earlier experience with Paper-Mate had proved this point.

One incident stands out in retrospect. While I was in Tokyo in January of 1958, during the contract negotiations, I received a call from one of my directors, who cautioned me against making any large commitment for radios. He had a point, since the market had become very soft; it was being flooded by thousands of radios similar in style, performance and appearance. The prices being asked were considerably lower than the SONY selling price. It was strongly suggested that I cut back on placing orders.

This was the time of decision. I was half-way around the world, in the midst of negotiations to conclude a contract. One of the plus factors was the orders I was going to place for delivery in 1958 on a month by month schedule of shipments.

It should be understood that, unless a commitment was made at least four to six months in advance, there could be no way of getting guaranteed delivery of the product. The SONY factory scheduled their orders on the production line. If orders were not programmed into their production, regardless of requirements, one could not get delivery of any radios until they had an open time. I decided to disregard this cautionary phone call, which was well meant, and take a calculated risk. I placed orders with the Tokyo factory for over 100,000 radios on a scheduled monthly delivery.

Happily, the demand exploded that year and we were the only company in Canada that had inventory and could deliver to our customers. We continued to advertise SONY strongly in all media, and the SONY name gained strength and recognition.

Going back to our contract negotiations, after the terms were agreed upon, both Morita and I signed the document. I told him that I would use it solely for our bankers, because we needed it to have our loans secured. After that, I would not look at it again, because what was required, more than anything else, was mutual trust. I asked if his photographer could be called in to take a picture of us shaking hands. This would mean more to me than any legal contract. He broke into a smile and readily agreed. This photograph is proudly displayed on the wall of my office and has been for the past 45-plus years.

It was late in 1957 that Morita and his associates, realizing that their destiny lay in the world arena, decided to change the name of Tokyo Tsushin Kogyo. They were looking for a short name, easily pronounced, and one that would be recognizable in all countries where their products would be sold. At the time they used, as a symbol, a smiling doll of a young boy that they called "Sonny Boy." In looking through a dictionary, Morita came across the Latin word *sonus*, meaning sound. He thought of the word "SONNY" for a small boy, which inspired him to drop one 'N', and so, the name SONY was born.

TOKYO TSUSHIN KOGYO WAS CHANGED AS THE

CORPORATE TITLE, AND SONY CORPORATION WAS

BORN TO BECOME THE LEGAL NAME OF THE COMPANY.

On May 13, 1959, as the decade was drawing to a close, a meeting was held in Winnipeg to review the family fortunes. Harry had been instrumental in moving us into the theatre exhibition business during and after the war. We had been operating four neighbourhood cinemas, two in Winnipeg, the Valour on Portage and Valour Road, and the Paris Theatre in St. Boniface. The other two were located in Calgary, the Crescent and Plaza theatres.

With the advent of television, business in neighbourhood theatres began to tail off rapidly, and by the early 1950s, all four theatres had been disposed of. This provided a source of capital which was loaned to the operating companies that had expanded considerably. The SONY business had created a need for capital, as all imports of the product were on a cash basis, against bills of lading. Duty, transportation, brokerage fees and the financing of our customers on a thirty- to sixty-day credit basis was a further drain on operating capital.

SAAN stores had expanded to a total of nineteen across the West, producing sales of $2,829,500 by the year ending December, 1959, with the chain being supported by the General Distributors guarantee to their sources of supply. Although the Bank of Nova Scotia, our principal banker at the time, had supported us, there was a limit to the credit available. All six brothers were married, with growing families, and required a higher standard of living.

At our meeting, we discussed expanding our operations and the possibilities of an acquisition. The total value of all assets was in the neighbourhood of $600,000. The question then came up as to what we should consider as an acquisition, and without giving it much thought I said, "You can't buy Woolworth's or Kresge's, but maybe we can acquire Metropolitan."

This spontaneous response was triggered because I had been shopping for an item usually found in a variety store a few days earlier. I had been at the Metropolitan Store, one of a chain, located on the corner of Portage Avenue and Carlton Street in Winnipeg, and the item was not available. I was struck by the poor lighting, the shoddy fixtures and the inadequate stock. When I went into Kresge's next door, the item was available. Their location was not as good as Metropolitan's, yet the store was efficiently laid out, nicely lit and well stocked.

My remark was not taken seriously by the brothers, because this sort of large acquisition did not seem to be within the realm of possibility. I decided, however, to take this idea a step further. On calling the Metropolitan Store, I asked to speak to the manager and was told his name was Ted Shaw. I asked Shaw the name of the president of the company, and he informed me that it was Joe Unger. He also informed me that Unger had recently been promoted to president of the H.L. Green Company and was now located in New York. On obtaining his address, I decided to write him a letter, requesting a meeting. His reply, the same week, was crisp and to the point: "For your information, it is not our intention to put Metropolitan up for sale."

Like many an event in my life and in the life of our company, the final result was quite different than anticipated.

The SONY Joint Venture

As the seventies began, our new 80,000 square foot headquarters, offices and processing warehouse were finally ready for occupation at 1370 SONY Place, in the Winnipeg suburb of Fort Garry. Although we moved in late 1970, it was on June 21, 1971, that Akio Morita of SONY Corporation, Tokyo, together with the Honourable Edward Schreyer, Premier of Manitoba, formally cut the ribbon to open the new premises.

This was the beginning of a fast paced expansion of SONY throughout all of Canada in the booming 1970s. In Toronto, SONY had operated out of third floor premises at 55 Wellington Street. The city of Toronto was in the midst of a tremendous building boom. When that building was sold, we bought a tract of land in a northern suburb of Toronto - then called Willowdale but today part of the GTA, or Greater Toronto Area and that building was officially opened on May 3, 1974. As the SONY line expanded and sales volume grew rapidly, we needed a new building in Montreal as well, to service Quebec and Atlantic Canada.

Brother Morley acquired 4 1/2 acres in suburban St. Laurent, and it was occupied by the spring of 1976.

One of the problems that we had to contend with was the fact that the company established as SONY of Canada, a division of SONY of America, was expanding at an ever-quicker pace. We were selling SONY consumer products through General Distributors, but were finding that there was a fine borderline between some of the products we were selling to schools, and what SONY of Canada was selling to the educational outlets they serviced.

It did not take long before the rumours started. My phone began to ring with inquiries by stock analysts, asking "when is SONY going to take over the distribution of all products in Canada?" It was common knowledge that SONY had taken over in France, forming SONY France; in Britain, they were known as SONY UK; in Germany as SONY GMBH; in Australia, SONY of Australia. Very few independent distributors of any size were still in existence, so why should Canada be any different?

Although General Distributors Ltd. continued to expand their sales in Canada, we could not help but be conscious of the presence of SONY of Canada Ltd. Koichi Tsunoda was appointed president of Socan, and he built a strong group of executives with engineering experience around him. This group, which was recruited through SONY of America, did nothing to dispel the rumours that they soon would be marketing the complete SONY line in Canada.

I reasoned that it was now time to talk to Morita about a joint venture. I was aware that it would be necessary to merge the two entities. It would be better to have 50 per cent of the *entire* SONY line, than risk the possibility of a non-renewal of our contract. My brothers and outside directors thought for sure that our company could never absorb SONY of Canada; I was told, *"Make any deal you can! Try and get 20 or 25 per cent equity! Be realistic! You'll never get 51 per cent!"* But I knew how deep my friendship was with Morita; I recalled how he shook hands with me and gave me his word of honour that we'd always have SONY in Canada. We had a special relationship; very unique, very different.

One of the more important moments in my career took place, by chance, when I took my family to Switzerland for an annual vacation, and befriended a person by the name of Kurt Lewin.

In 1972, the Nixon administration decided that the US would go off the gold standard, a major step that would affect currencies around the world. One evening, I spoke with my friend Kurt about this move, and its impact on the countries I worked with the most.

Kurt was aware that our company was the distributor for SONY consumer products for all of Canada, and we discussed how the Japanese yen might react; it was then valued at 360 to the Canadian dollar.

"If you could buy any yen currency at the prevailing prices, you'd be well ahead of the game," he advised me. In his opinion, the yen would probably be revalued at about 300 yen to the Canadian dollar, which was valuable information for Gendis! The yen was a controlled currency, and could not be bought on the open market, so it seemed unlikely that I could use this information to the advantage of General Distributors. We would simply have to raise prices on the SONY products that we were importing from Japan.

The following day, my family and I flew back to Canada, stopping in Toronto to get over the jet lag. After we settled in at the Four Seasons

Inn on the Park, I phoned Bill Nicks, the Chairman and CEO of the Bank of Nova Scotia and a close friend, after all our years of working together. He had investigated the possibility of opening a branch in Tokyo upon my urging, and was keenly aware of the emerging Japanese economy. The bank followed up with opening branches in Hong Kong and a number of Middle East countries.

Visiting Bill in his office, I shared the information I had received from my friend Kurt Lewin, and his belief that the yen would be revalued within days. I added that I was disappointed that the Japanese currency was not traded on any money market, so that I might take advantage of this important currency shift.

"Do you have orders placed with SONY for future delivery?" Nicks asked me.

"Of course I do!" I smiled. "I have to place purchases at least six months in advance, as SONY has been growing so rapidly. Why, if I failed to have orders placed for fall and Christmas, the height of the season, we wouldn't be able to get delivery of our SONY products."

"What's the amount of the orders placed?"

"Approximately $4 to $5 million," I replied.

"It's true that you can't buy yen for speculation, but you *can* forward payment in advance for your orders. We can do this through the Mitsui Bank in New York, who would then transfer the funds to SONY in Tokyo. I'd better call my VP in charge of currencies, and let's have a discussion on this."

The man was Cedric Ritchie, a future CEO of the bank. After we discussed Bill Nicks' plan, Bill called the Mitsui Bank in New York. He advised them that they were to transfer $5 million to the credit of SONY Corporation Tokyo for credit of the General Distributors Limited account. All this was accomplished in one phone call!

When this deal was complete, I could not resist expressing my surprise.

"Bill, you realize that you've just increased my line of credit by over $4 million, as my line in Winnipeg is approximately $1 million!"

"I'll take care of that, Albert," Nicks laughed.

Naturally, I was most appreciative of the confidence that Bill Nicks had in Gendis, after all, he had more than quintupled our credit, with a single stroke of the pen.

Nicks then decided to phone George Korinaga, the Manager of the Bank of Nova Scotia branch in Tokyo, to tell him to follow up with information to SONY and its executives.

"Bill, it's 3 a.m. Saturday morning in Tokyo! You'll wake him from a deep sleep!" I said.

"Good," said Nicks. "We'll wake him and make him aware of what we've done to help his branch of the bank in Tokyo increase his volume!"

And so it all took place, time differences notwithstanding: the sleepy Tokyo bank manager was woken up, told that SONY would be credited with $5 million prepayment of SONY merchandise for the account of General Distributors Limited. I asked to speak to Korinaga and told him to phone Akio Morita at home with this important information but not before 7:30 a.m.! And thus, SONY Japan was credited with the $5 million to the Gendis account.

When I returned to Winnipeg, I was criticized by several of my directors for what had transpired at my meeting with Bill Nicks and Cedric Ritchie.

*"Do you mean to tell us that you transferred $5 million to the credit of SONY from General Distributors Limited **without** a note signed by Mr. Morita or one of that company's principals?"*

"Look," I explained, "if we were going to get the appreciation of the yen, then action had to be taken at once!"

Yet, that Monday, there was nothing in the financial newspapers about any change in the value of the yen, which remained at 360 to the Canadian dollar. Each day that week was the same: no change!

A week later, however, it was announced: the yen had been revalued to 320 to the Canadian dollar and, within months, there was further appreciation in the value of the yen to 280 to our dollar.

What had we gained by the forward purchase of the yen? We now did not have to raise prices on SONY products, whereas our competitors, who handled other Japanese electronics, had to raise their prices almost immediately.

Probably the most important benefit from this decision was that I enhanced the confidence that Akio Morita had in our Canadian company. Two weeks after this all occurred, I visited Akio in Tokyo.

"What premium are you expecting from SONY with that $5 million dollar transfer to our account, Albert?" Morita asked me.

"Akio, I am not looking for anything more than the interest that we are paying for the money which was advanced to SONY."

He smiled, and I knew that he was exceedingly pleased in the confidence and trust that I had in the SONY Corporation.

I was not aware at that time that Morita was negotiating with the Japanese banks with which he was dealing. Among the Japanese business conglomerates, he was seen as a maverick; there was little love lost for this outspoken Japanese personality who frequently took his fellow-citizens to task for their archaic business methods. I heard, only afterwards, what that transfer of $5 million to the account of SONY Corporation meant to the company. They were actually in the act of negotiations with the Mitsui Bank and Tokyo Bank for an additional line of credit and my rather daring, precipitous actions helped SONY in their negotiation at that time.

But how to approach Morita, when we still had six years to go on the most recent contract, which he had given us as a concession? I decided that a direct approach was the best way, and I arranged a meeting with him in Tokyo. We discussed frankly the problems that had arisen since SONY of Canada Ltd. had been established. I pointed out that we had always cooperated, and that I had his word we would always have distribution rights in Canada. I explained the confusion in the marketplace, where two different companies were calling on the same account, with some of the same SONY products. There was an overlapping, in some cases, of the professional and educational products. Gendis was still distributing the educational products to some of the universities and schools, while Socan was selling professional products to these same accounts.

Morita listened to my presentation and said, "Albert, I gave you a ten year contract recently, which still has five years to go, and now you are asking for a new deal. We are a large company today, and I will have to go to my board of directors if you have a proposition to present. It may be difficult, but present your suggestions the next time we meet."

At least I did not have a refusal. It was up to me to work out something fair to both our companies. And so, the next time we met, I presented a plan where we would have an exchange of Gendis shares for SONY Corporation of Tokyo shares. I left the proposal with Morita for consideration. Within a couple of months he advised me this could not be accomplished, due to Japanese restrictions on the exchange of shares.

My next proposal was probably geared too strongly in favour of General Distributors, and again I received a thumbs down on the joint venture proposal. I then asked Morita if *he* could come up with a proposal, and he said that it was most difficult, and that the onus was on me. I would have to make the proposal acceptable to his board of directors.

In the meantime, the fortunes of SONY Corporation, Tokyo, were growing at a blistering pace. Distributor after distributor was being bought out and taken over, and one of the first distributors in the US, Superscope Inc., was in a legal dispute with SONY Corporation. The times were not conducive to negotiations for a joint venture agreement with Canada.

The story of how Akio Morita broke with that early distributor could fill several chapters of its own, as it reflects on how crucial friendship and simple human decency are, to achieve business success. Joe Tushinsky and his two brothers handled hi-fi products and were specialists in that. They met Akio, saw one of his tape recorders, and began to handle it in the U.S. As SONY's growth exploded around the world, Tushinsky feared that the Japanese firm would break with him, so he asked for another contract.

Because I knew of the negotiations between SONY and Superscope, I asked Morita if he was renewing the Superscope contract.

"I knew the contract was coming to an end, and I had no reason to renew it," Morita told me.

"What turned you off so much?" I queried.

Morita replied: "They wanted to renew the contract, so I brought Ed Rosiny, my New York based lawyer, along with me, and went to their offices in California."

When we walked into the office together, Joe asked, *"Who's that with you?"*

Morita replied, "This is Ed Rosiny, and you've met him before; he's my lawyer. I want him to attend this meeting."

"Well, I'm not having a meeting with your lawyer!" Tushinsky declared, "I invited YOU to have a meeting."

I knew Joe Tushinsky, and he *was* a pompous fellow, who clearly lacked the savoir faire to deal with a sensitive Japanese entrepreneur like Akio Morita. And so, the Tushinsky family, and SuperScope their firm, soon parted company with SONY, which chose not to renew the contract.

There is an interesting ending to the story: Ed Rosiny, SONY's lawyer, was brought in once more, this time to buy up the inventory. He coldly noted to Tushinsky that "We're not renewing your contract, and your inventory isn't worth what you paid for it, since it's old inventory now!"

Morita had agreed to buy it up for $200,000 but Rosiny told Morita he would do the negotiation, "I'll do better for you." he promised.

Rosiny eventually managed to purchase all the old inventory from Superscope for a mere $80,000. He told the SONY chairman what he had accomplished and he added, "I'm not charging you one penny for my negotiation!" Rosiny proved to Morita that he was able to save SONY a considerable amount of money through his negotiation.

Early in March, 1973, I received a call from Harvey Schein, the newly appointed president of SONY of America, that he wished to visit me in Winnipeg. When I asked him the purpose of his visit, he told me that he had authority from Akio Morita to negotiate a joint venture agreement with General Distributors on behalf of SONY Corporation, Tokyo. I advised him that the only person I would negotiate with was Akio Morita. If he wished to visit Winnipeg to see our operation as an associate, all courtesies would be extended, but unless he had a letter addressed to me, authorizing him to negotiate on behalf of SONY, Tokyo, I was not ready to have any discussions with him on this subject. When Schein visited Winnipeg, I showed him all the courtesies but my negotiations continued with Morita and Rosiny.

Therefore, back to square one: how to negotiate a joint venture to our mutual benefit? Enter Ed Rosiny, chief negotiator for SONY on their many joint ventures with international companies. He had negotiated a 50/50 joint venture with the Columbia Broadcasting System to manufacture and sell CBS records in Japan and throughout Asia; a 50/50 joint venture with Union Carbide to manufacture and sell Eveready batteries throughout Japan and the Far East; and a 50/50 joint venture with TEKTRONIX, Inc. to manufacture and sell oscilloscopes and other precision measuring devices in Japan and Asia. Now it was his turn to negotiate a joint venture with General Distributors of Canada, which, no doubt, he would attempt to structure to the benefit of SONY, Tokyo. It was up to me to match wits with Rosiny, and protect our interests.

Ed Rosiny was raised in the east side of New York. Standing about five feet, two inches in height, Rosiny was slight of build and of hypersensitive temperament. A little Bonaparte, he smoked incessantly and had a booming voice that belied his appearance: one expected such a noise to come out of a much *larger* person. Indeed, most would associate such a voice with a tall, portly individual with an aggressive personality. Despite his appearance, Rosiny could overwhelm you with his aggressiveness, if you were not prepared. In our first meeting, which took place in Tokyo, I advised him that I wished to talk with Morita personally. I sensed a coldness and a defensive attitude from Morita that was never there in our previous meetings.

It was not surprising that Morita had become wary of the on-going negotiations between our two firms, in spite of our friendly relations. As our negotiations progressed during the few days I met with Rosiny in Tokyo, I had sensed that this was so. At all times, Rosiny kept me from any further direct meetings with Morita, feeling that my long-time friend was giving me too many concessions. I knew that Rosiny was interested in building his own prestige with Morita to further his interests, and that all my negotiations would have to be directed through him.

Rosiny's association with SONY went back to when he was the lawyer acting on behalf of a firm to which Morita had given the exclusive distribution for SONY radios back in 1956. When the contract expired, SONY opened their first overseas operation, a wholly-owned subsidiary, SONY Corporation of America, at 514 Broadway. As SONY flourished, Rosiny was retained as counsel for SONY of America, and his actions became more and more important. He had clearly earned Morita's confidence in his ability to act in the best interests of the SONY Corporation.

After I left Tokyo and on my return to Winnipeg, I decided that it was in our company's best interest to engage the services of G.R. (Dick) Hunter, of Pitblado & Hoskins, to act on our behalf in further negotiations. In his work on the acquisition of Metropolitan from H.L. Green in 1961, Dick had proved his mettle, and I had full confidence in his ability to act on our behalf. I had a number of telephone conversations with Rosiny, and felt a wide barrier being raised between Morita and myself. He continued to insist that I was *not* to engage in any direct contacts with Morita, yet I continued to hang tough, arguing that all our previous deals had been made on a one-to-one basis.

In our first discussion, it was contemplated between Rosiny and me that the joint venture company would operate under the corporate name of Gendis SONY Ltd. However, after giving the matter considerable thought, I felt the connotation of this name would be that we were still acting as a distributor, and department stores and large accounts prefer to deal directly with the manufacturer. Therefore, I felt that SONY of Canada Ltd. should be the name of the joint venture. Rosiny argued that Morita would not agree to having the corporate name SONY owned by any other group, but I prevailed upon him to make my wishes known to Morita. Rosiny was surprised when Morita agreed to my proposal.

I argued for 51 per cent ownership by General Distributors and 49 per cent SONY, Tokyo. Again, Rosiny said that Morita would not agree.

Finally, an agreement on this matter was reached. The deal was that General Distributors would own 51 per cent of the newly merged company; SONY Corporation, Tokyo, 49 per cent. Akio Morita agreed to this formula. The deal was signed and concluded in Winnipeg, to go into effect as of February 1, 1975, and Morita attended a dinner in Toronto to commemorate the signing.

AKIO MORITA
PRESIDENT

SONY
SONY CORPORATION

7-35 KITASHINAGAWA-6
SHINAGAWA-KU, TOKYO 141, JAPAN
TELEPHONE: (03) 448-2002
CABLE ADDRESS:
SONYCORP TOKYO
TELEX: J 22262

February 6, 1975

Mr. Albert D. Cohen
President
General Distributors of Canada Ltd.
1370 Sony Place, Fort Garry
Winnipeg 19
Canada

Dear Albert:

Thank you very much for your letter of January 28. I, too, am very happy that after twenty years our two companies are finally being consummated in a permanent relationship.

It is my great pleasure to learn that you are planning to extend your visit to Hawaii to Tokyo. I shall be very happy to welcome you on March 25. At present, my schedule, as well as Iwama and Ohga's, are fairly open at that time, and I am hoping that business won't take us away from Tokyo during your visit.

Looking forward to seeing you again then.

With kindest regards,

Sincerely yours,

Akio

AM:ts

The joint venture with SONY Corporation was a tremendous accomplishment. **Canada is the only western country in which SONY had a joint venture; everywhere else, it operated with wholly owned subsidiaries.** For all time, General Distributors had exclusivity of SONY products for all of Canada - a fact which lasted until we sold our 51% back to SONY of Japan in the mid-90s.

Although the rumours of a take-over by SONY of General Distributors were laid to rest by the announcement of the joint venture, the question of the integration of the two entities still had to be thrashed out. SONY Tokyo was anxious to move the marketing headquarters to Toronto. I cautioned Morita that it would take at least a few years to accomplish this. I agreed that Toronto was the logical place for the operational headquarters, because 70 per cent of our country's population was in central and eastern Canada. But to try and rush this transition would be harmful. It was very important to gain the confidence of the merged division personnel, so that they would know we were working toward a common goal: the growth of SONY of Canada.

The growth of sales of SONY of Canada Ltd. were quite extraordinary, since the signing of the joint venture.

Furthermore, I felt gratified that Akio Morita, in the closing and signing of our joint venture, had referred to the friendship and gratitude for work that had been done on behalf of the SONY Corporation, and the fact that SONY had used Canada as a training ground for Japanese executives now operating out of many SONY subsidiaries around the world.

Universal and Disney Sue SONY

In the early 1970s, sales of colour television sets were booming. The Shadow-Mask system, developed by RCA, had been licensed as a basic patent to manufacturers around the world. In the United States alone, the potential was for sales in the neighbourhood of twenty million sets. This was a market that SONY was not participating in, because Ibuka felt that being a licencee of RCA would put SONY in the same category as all other manufacturers. Therefore, Ibuka decided to develop a superior system that would be exclusive to SONY. The fact that other giants in the electronic field Philips, General Electric, Westinghouse and others, had tried and been unsuccessful did not deter Ibuka from blazing this new trail for SONY.

Ibuka set up a research and development team that worked around the clock to try and develop a colour television tube that would be superior in performance to the triple-gun RCA Shadow Mask. There was great wailing from the SONY subsidiaries and distributors, who felt they were losing a huge opportunity by not being able to supply their accounts with a SONY colour television set, and argued constantly that SONY should obtain a licence from RCA. But Ibuka was insistent that his team continue in their research to develop a tube on their own.

Towards the end of 1966, a young engineer by the name of Miyaoka, while experimenting with a single gun and three cathodes, made a happy mistake that produced a blurred picture. He reported his results to his superior, Yoshida. When Ibuka heard the results of Miyaoka's experiment, he declared, "This is what I have been waiting for. Miyaoka has come up with the solution. We will put all our efforts behind this principle." Instead of the thousands of dots of the RCA system, SONY developed the now famous one-gun Trinitron colour patented tube.

This gave tremendous impetus to the growth of SONY in the 1970s; the 1980s would receive the glory of the Walkman. To give the reader an idea of the importance of Trinitron, by 1976 SONY had sold ten million sets. In 1977, production was scheduled at two million sets per month.

New factories at Inazawa and Ichinomiya were working around the clock to try and supply the ever increasing world demand for the dazzlingly superior SONY Trinitron.

The seeds of the home video recorder were also sown in this decade. Even though CBS had lost over $30 million in experimenting to produce electronic video recording, and Ampex had been unsuccessful in their attempts to produce a home video unit, and another firm, Cartridge Television, had lost over $60 million in attempting to develop a home unit, SONY continued to plow ahead with their experiments in this field.

By 1960, SONY engineers produced their first important videotape recorder. Although it did not achieve the visual fidelity of an earlier Ampex machine, its price was barely more than a tenth of the Ampex $100,000 VTR, so its effect on the market was great. A number of National Football League teams used it to study their practices; airlines began to use the sets to show take-offs and landings to their passengers. By 1964, SONY put out a second VTR, selling for around $3,000, followed by another version the following year, at $1,200. By 1966, the first low priced, compact videotape recorder hit the market at only $800. From the very beginning, SONY's goal was inspired: to create a unit which would be used primarily in homes.

The advantage that SONY always had was that they were leaders in VTR (videotape recording) technology through their development of the U-matic VTR, a one inch recording system sold primarily for commercial and educational use. It was with the intention of having one system, that Morita made available the SONY technology to the Matsushita Corporation. Morita felt strongly that even though Matsushita was a larger and stronger company financially, at that time by having one system, SONY would gain a greater share of the market as the SONY brand was better known throughout the world.

Although SONY was the first to introduce the Betamax to the consumer market, the mammoth Matsushita Corporation, through their controlled subsidiary, Japan Victor Company (JVC), introduced a competitive non-compatible system, VHS. The battle was on! SONY had the advantage of being first on the market, but made the mistake of providing only one hour of playing time, against two hours on the JVC machine.

Although the SONY Betamax was a superior product which produced a better picture on the television screen, the public were more interested in a lower price and longer playing time. When SONY produced a new Betamax model which *could* produce two hour playing time, JVC shot back with a four hour tape.

Slowly, the market began to expand, as the public became aware of this new "time shift" product, which gave users the opportunity to view TV programs at their own convenience.

In Canada, with the many new products being produced by SONY, sales exploded, growing from $11,895,000 in 1969 to $85,519,000 in 1979. Joint-venture sales after 1975 included all SONY products, while before that, sales were for consumer products only.

Many years later, in 1974, Schreiber mentioned to me that MCA was working on a new invention called Discovision. It was a method of video recording on records that would be played back and projected on a TV screen. Universal's interest was that it would be a method of selling movies to homes in the same way that long-playing records (LPs) sold, through their Decca division. Schreiber and MCA were most excited about this new medium, and Schreiber invited me to attend a demonstration. He wanted to know if SONY would be interested in manufacturing the Discovision hardware, for which they would supply the software. I told him that I would make inquiries on his behalf.

Many meetings followed, along with numerous calls between Winnipeg, Hollywood, Tokyo and New York. Morita and his associates made a number of trips, and seriously considered whether SONY should become involved in a joint venture with MCA.

If SONY found itself in a struggle between the Beta and VHS system, there is a lesser-known example of SONY wisdom. It had to do with my own personal friendship with Taft Schreiber, whom I had first met in Japan in 1959, when he was president of Revue Studios and vice-president of MCA, the parent company of Universal Studios of Hollywood. I assisted him in obtaining contacts with the Japanese, with whom he wished to establish a branch of Revue.

At this time, I was in my *own* negotiations with Morita on the SONY of Canada joint venture, as mentioned earlier. One day in New York, I asked Morita if he was serious about concluding a deal with MCA. His answer was that it was an interesting new approach to video recording, and the hand-made samples produced an excellent picture. But he finally stated, "Albert, *we* are the world leaders in videotape technology. Therefore, we will concentrate on what we know best." "Besides," he observed, "You can produce an excellent duplication from a matrix but the quality falls off rapidly if you want to produce thousands to sell to the public."

The wisdom of Morita's judgment was proven in future years. Eventually, MCA finalized a joint venture with Philips of the Netherlands after SONY decided against joining MCA. Discovision cost over $30 million in development, and it never did become a commercial consumer success. Yet SONY and Philips have successfully developed and marketed the new compact audio disc technology, which offers remarkable digitally-encoded sound.

But this did not come without a quite extraordinary court case, with me being called as a witness, speaking as the president of SONY of Canada, Ltd., and some rather stellar plaintiffs who were suing SONY, along with some of their retail distributors in the United States: Universal City Studios, Inc., Universal Television and Universal Pictures, all subsidiaries of MCA, and Walt Disney Corporation. I was clearly in good company! But then, I was being represented by two lawyers, one of whom was Frank Rosiny, Ed Rosiny's son, who became a partner in his father's law firm.

The deposition, which was taken "in the informal setting of a conference room" in Winnipeg, had the same force and effect as if I had been testifying in a court of law, so I spoke under oath. My reminiscences were extremely important to SONY, since the challenge was certainly a major one: *were these new-fangled VTRs (Video Tape Recorders) which were now flooding the market—the date was early June, 1978—going to damage the earnings of such giant studios as Universal and Disney?* After all, it was clear that the machines would allow home taping, which could apparently deny the Hollywood studios millions, even billions, of dollars in revenue.

As I look over the 96-page deposition, nearly a quarter-century later, I am surprised by the angry outbursts, the flashes of sarcasm and humor, but, most critically, how much my words and relationship with Taft Schreiber would damage the case of Universal and Disney.

SONY Judgement in Favour of Betamax

IN 1979, THE UNITED STATES DISTRICT COURT IN
CALIFORNIA AWARDED ITS JUDGEMENT IN
FAVOUR OF THE SONY CORPORATION.

The Deposition and examination held in Winnipeg resulted in a victory for SONY in hearing of the United States District Court in California.

There is no question that the correspondence between Taft Schreiber and myself was the evidence that on the examination by the California judge helped result in a decision in favour of SONY.

The reason for the case brought by Universal and Disney was easy to understand because time proved it was a very shortsighted attempt to ban recordings off the air. They believed that movies that were beginning to be shown on television would be recorded on VHS or Betamax and it would mean a loss of revenue for the studios. Universal had bought a company in which one of the assets was Discovision.

This equipment had the capability of playback but could not record off the air. Disney and Universal thought that by controlling Discovision, they could sell their movies to the public who would buy their Discovision machines. In this manner, they would have a monopoly.

Time proved that you cannot stop progress and new electronic marvels. Instead of one million machines, which Universal in their mistaken belief would open a new outlet for their movies in just a few years, there were over one hundred million video recorders sold world-wide. Not only did this open a new market for Universal and all the other movie studios to sell their libraries of old movies but Disney prospered more than any of the studios because *their* inventory of old movies became priceless. SONY led the way. As of this date of publication, there is over a billion recorders of all makes that have been sold world wide.

Movies like Snow White, Cinderella and all the other classics became timeless. As each new generation of children came of age, these movies were released every few years to excellent success. It was ironic that they were fighting the enemy windmills – an enemy that did not exist. SONY the innovators who were shamelessly copied by their competitors, went it all alone for a victory that benefited all the manufacturers of video recorders.

Following is some of the correspondence between myself and Taft Schreiber which is referred to in the deposition.

In retrospect, it was fortunate that in a conversation that Akio Morita mentioned to me when we were having a private dinner that he was concerned about the trial where a decision would be made on the lawsuit by Universal and Disney re Betamax. I mentioned the extensive correspondence that I had with Taft Schreiber.

SONY had spent millions in defending the lawsuit. I asked Morita if Panasonic or any other Japanese firm were contributing to help in the cost which if successful, would benefit the whole industry.

Morita said, "Albert, we have not been offered any help from any of the other manufacturers, we are going it alone and it is quite a burden".

I promised Morita at the time that when I returned from Tokyo, I would examine my private file of correspondence with Taft Schreiber. The result was a series of letters between us that substantiated that not only did Universal know of the Betamax and its capabilities but Universal was anxious to obtain a number of the Betamax machines for their own purposes.

There is no doubt that it was my testimony that was of assistance in the judgement in favour of SONY.

100 UNIVERSAL CITY PLAZA
UNIVERSAL CITY, CALIFORNIA 91608

PHONE 985-4321

EXECUTIVE OFFICES

December 18, 1969

Mr. Albert D. Cohen
General Distributors Ltd.
791 Notre Dame Avenue
Winnipeg 3, Canada

Dear Mr. Cohen:

I do not think that the novelty of three television sets in one is
sufficiently great to excite the public, but I do believe that if
somebody would put all seven stations available in the major
markets into one set, it would create a tremendous amount of
free publicity.

I have just returned from the hospital where I had some minor
surgery, and I am now recuperating at home.

In the meantime, I want to tell you how nice it was meeting you
in New York, and I do hope we will have some mutual interests
in which we can both benefit in the future.

With best wishes, I am,

Yours very sincerely,

Jules Stein
Chairman of the Board

JCS:gh

November 10th, 1969.

Mr. Taft B. Schreiber,
Universal Pictures,
445 Park Ave.,
New York, N. Y.,
U. S. A.

Dear Taft:

Enclosed please find a xerox copy of a letter
sent by Mr. Rosiny to your address in California which
I am not sure if you will have received. The letter
is self-explanatory.

I will be arriving in New York the evening
of Sunday, November 16th, and will call you at your
office on the 17th.

I look forward however to seeing you at the
Essex House at Mr. Morita's suite at 5:00 p. m. Certainly bring along as many of your associates as you
would like to.

I look forward to the pleasure of seeing you
and with kindest personal regards, I am,

Yours very truly,

Albert D. Cohen

ADC:SB

Encl.

100 UNIVERSAL CITY PLAZA
UNIVERSAL CITY, CALIFORNIA 91608

PHONE 985-4321

EXECUTIVE OFFICES

May 3, 1974

Mr. Albert D. Cohen
President
General Distributors Limited
1370 Sony Place
Winnipeg, Manitoba
Canada

Dear Albert:

Mr. Mobuchi and his associates saw the demonstration of
our Discovision. They were enormously impressed. Mobuchi
had to go back but Mr. Oniki came back for a second
meeting and then was taken to our laboratory and told us
that his people were even more impressed after what they
saw in the lab. I don't know what will happen from the
Sony interests. I appreciate your attempting to bring us
together and it may be fruitful.

There are major companies that are seriously in negotiation
with us but nothing yet has been consummated in connection
with a joint venture manufacturing operation, which is
principally what we have in mind.

There are various alternatives open to us involving the
manufacture of hardware. One option is joining together
in some kind of cooperative effort with one of the major
companies that have electronic manufacturing facilities
"in place". On balance, that may be the more intelligent
approach and we have been having, and are now having, serious
discussions with several of these "household name" companies
who have contacted us with that objective in mind. We are
still in the decision making process in that regard, electing
not to rush precipitately into something which involves a
long term relationship.

Every good wish.

Sincerely,

Taft B. Schreiber

TBS:eb

100 UNIVERSAL CITY PLAZA
UNIVERSAL CITY, CALIFORNIA 91608

PHONE 985-4321

EXECUTIVE OFFICES

May 15, 1974

Mr. Albert D. Cohen
General Distributors Limited
1370 Sony Place, Fort Garry
Winnipeg 19, Canada

Dear Albert:

Thank you for the Creative Strategies Incorporated
Sony review. This is a remarkable document and
I am grateful that you have sent it.to me. I am
sending it to the pertinent people here to read.

I hope all continues to go well with you.

Best regards,

Taft B. Schreiber

TBS:eb

December 12, 1975.

Taft B. Schreiber, Esq.,
President,
Revue Studios,
Universal City, California,
U. S. A.

Dear Taft;

You will be interested in knowing that our joint venture has its' official closing in Winnipeg on Tuesday, December 16th.

I am enclosing an analysis of our company by Richardson Securities which may be of interest, particularly to the remarks pertaining to Betamax.

Trusting that all is well with you and may I take this opportunity of wishing you the very best of the holiday season.

Yours sincerely,

Albert D. Cohen

ADC:MR

Encl.

IOO UNIVERSAL CITY PLAZA
UNIVERSAL CITY, CALIFORNIA 91608

PHONE 985-4321

EXECUTIVE OFFICES

December 18, 1975

Mr. Albert D. Cohen
General Distributors of Canada Ltd.
1370 Sony Place, Fort Garry
Winnipeg, Canada   R3C 3C3

Dear Albert:

We are off to Hawaii on the 19th and I will be at the Kahala Hilton
for three weeks this year.

Congratulations on the official closing of your deal with Sony.
I am sure it's constructive for you, your family, the stockholders
and Sony.

The Richardson Report is quite interesting and certainly there is
a market for "Betamax". I hope that it contributes importantly
to your earnings. We are coming along quite well with Discovision
and it should be on the market the fall or the end of 1976.
There are two different instruments of course, and ours really is
for the future of video-audio combined for home use as an extension
of the record album market. We are optimistic but it's going to be
the public that will tell the story.

With all good wishes for the coming year in which Rita joins me.

Sincerely,

Taft B. Schreiber

100 UNIVERSAL CITY PLAZA
UNIVERSAL CITY, CALIFORNIA 91608

PHONE 985-4321

EXECUTIVE OFFICES

April 26, 1976

Mr. Albert D. Cohen
President & Chief Executive Officer
General Distributors of Canada Ltd.
1370 Sony Place
Winnipeg, Manitoba R3C 3C3
Canada

Dear Albert:

I have the annual reports of Metropolitan Stores and
General Distributors and again they are a model of
efficiency and growth. You should be very proud of
all that you have accomplished.

We are having lunch with Mr. Morita today and I will
tell him I have seen your reports and complimented
you on them.

Best regards,

Taft B. Schreiber

<u>PERSONAL</u>   March 9, 1978

Mr. Akio Morita
Sony Corporation of America
9 West 57th Avenue
NEW YORK, N. Y. 10019
U. S. A.

Dear Akio:

   I received a phone call from Mr. Frank Rosiny
where he inquired if I had any correspondence that might
be of assistance to you in the MCA case.

   I related to him my close relationship and the
many telephone conversations that we had on the subject
of Betamax and Videodisc. I also related to him how I
tried to bring the Sony Corporation together with MCA on
this subject matter. He asked me to look through my files
to see if I had any correspondence that would be of assistance. The enclosed letter dated December 28th, of which
I have the original in my files, is self-explanatory. When
I read the letter to Frank Rosiny, he felt that the third
paragraph of the letter would be of tremendous assistance.
I was also able to make available the Richardson Securities
Report on our Company and I read to him the items on Betamax
on page 4 and on the Videodisc on page 5 which also, he
feels, would be of assistance.

   I will be at the Kahala Hilton in Hawaii from
March 18th with my wife and the two younger children for
at least two weeks. By coincidence, Frank Rosiny will be
there for a few days from March 17th and he requested some
time so that we could discuss the various telephone conversations that I had with Taft Schreiber.

               ....../2

          - 2 -

   I thought that the information would be of
interest to you.

    Kindest personal regards,

      Yours Sincerely

ADC:NL   ALBERT D. COHEN

Enclosures

Following is an excerpt from the United States District Court Judgement:

UNIVERSAL CITY STUDIOS v. SONY CORP. OF AMERICA
Cite as 480 F.Supp.429 (1979)

UNIVERSAL CITY STUDIOS, INC., a corporation, dba Universal Television and Universal Pictures, and Walt Disney Productions, a corporation, Plaintiffs,

v.

SONY CORPORATION OF AMERICA, a corporation, the SONY Corporation, a corporation, Carter Hawley Hale Stores, Inc., a corporation, Associated Dry Goods Corporation, a corporation, Federated Department Stores, Inc., a corporation, Henry's Camera Corporation, a corporation, Doyle Dane Bernbach, Inc., a corporation, and William Griffiths, Defendants.

No. CV76-3520-F

United States District Court, C.D. California
Oct. 2, 1979.
As Amended Dec. 5, 1979.

Owners of copyrighted audiovisual materials brought infringement action against manufacturers, distributors, retailers and advertisers of videotape recorder. The District Court, Ferguson, J., held that:

(1) *copyright holders of audiovisual materials, some of which were sold for telecast over public airwaves, did not have monopoly power over off-the-air copying of those materials by owners of video tape recorder in their homes for private, noncommercial use;*

(2) *retailer did not infringe upon copyrights where it did not compete with nor profit from materials and intended only to demonstrate recorder;*

(3) *even if home-use copying constituted infringement, neither manufacturers, distributors, retailers, nor advertisers were liable under theories of direct or contributory infringement or vicarious liability; and*

(4) *even if they were deemed liable, injunctive relief was not available where they did not unfairly compete with owners of copyrighted materials nor interfere with their advantageous business relations.*

JUDGEMENT FOR DEFENDANTS.

Following are excerpts taken from the Supreme Court Reporter:

SUPREME COURT REPORTER

Owners of copyrights on television programs brought copyright infringement action against manufacturers of home video tape recorders. The United States District Court for the Central District of California, 480F.Supp.429, denied all relief sought by copyright owners and entered judgement for manufacturers, and owners appealed. The United States Court of Appeals for the Ninth Circuit, 659 F.2d 963, reversed district court's judgement on copyright claim, and manufacturers petitioned for writ of certiorari. The Supreme Court, Justice Stevens, held that manufacturers of home videotape recorders demonstrated a significant likelihood that substantial numbers of copyright holders who licensed their works for broadcast on free television would not object to having their broadcasts time shifted by private viewers and owners of copyrights on television programs failed to demonstrate that time shifting would cause any likelihood of nonminimal harm to the potential market for, or the value of, their copy-righted works and therefore home videotape recorder was capable of substantial noninfringing uses; thus, manufacturers' sale of such equipment to general public did not constitute contributory infringement of respondents' copyrights.

The introduction of the home videotape recorder (VTR) upon the market has enabled millions of Americans to make recordings of television programs in their homes, for future and repeated viewing at their own convenience. While this practice has proved highly popular with owners of television sets and VTR's, it understandably has been a matter of concern for the holders of copyrights in the recorded programs. A result is the present litigation, raising the issues whether the home recording of a copyrighted television program is an infringement of the copyright, and, if so, whether the manufacturers and distributors of VTR's are liable as contributory infringers. I would hope that these questions ultimately will be considered seriously and in depth by the Congress and be resolved there, despite the fact that the Court's decision today provides little incentive for congressional action. Our task in the meantime, however, is to resolve these issues as best we can in the light of ill-fitting existing copyright law.

After a 5-week trial, the District Court, with a detailed opinion, ruled that home VTR recording did not infringe the Studios' copyrights.

The District Court also held that even if home VTR recordings were an infringement, SONY could not be held liable under theories of direct infringement, contributory infringement, or vicarious liability. Finally, the court concluded that an injunction against sales of the Betamax would be inappropriate even if SONY were liable under on or more of those theories.

480 F.Supp. 429 (1979)

Jogging into the Eighties
with the Walkman

The company now had the diversification and safety nets that I was trying to create, so that we would not be too dependent on any one sales season, or any one facet of our business. As General Distributors moved steadily into the eighties, the three retail chains, Metropolitan, Greenberg's and SAAN, were growing and prospering. The A.L. Green chain had been absorbed into Greenberg's and Metropolitan, and that acquisition, with the closing of some of the non-profitable stores, was beginning to pay benefits and carry its own weight. Further economies of scale had been affected by consolidating the Greenberg warehouse into the A.L. Green warehouse, which had sufficient space to house the enlarged Greenberg operation. Indeed, our consolidating did not stop with warehouses; if one walked into a Greenberg store in the province of Quebec without noticing the sign, he or she would assume that it was a SAAN. The fact that we opened thirty-six new stores in 1984 alone, gives a suggestion of our success during that period.

SONY, as always, continually expanded its innovative product line. Betamax sales continued to grow. Then, a new product, the SONY Walkman, created a sensation. The story of how this came about is of interest.

Back in 1978, Mr. Ibuka, who traveled extensively by plane, was not satisfied with the bulky earphones and the music offered to the passengers through a central control. He therefore asked his engineers to take one of the SONY portable tape recorders, and shrink it into a play-back unit only. This was done, and with some pre-recorded CBS SONY tapes, he was able to enjoy his next plane trip more, listening to the music of his choice. Next, he asked to have very lightweight earphones made, and therefore, a new personal and portable hi-fi product emerged, born of Ibuka's necessity. He turned it over to his sales department and serenely suggested that "there might be a market for this item."

Akio Morita, an avid tennis player, saw the product and used it while on the court. He discovered that it helped with the rhythm of his stroke, and quickly decided that it had massive sales potential. Yasuo Kuroki was assigned to develop this new product, which was given the inspired name of the Walkman.

When the SONY of America president and his buying team, together with our SONY of Canada buyers, attended a conference in which Akio Morita enthusiastically introduced the Walkman, SONY of America was asked how many the New York office was ready to purchase. Seeing the enthusiasm of Morita, the spokesman for the group decided to go way out; he said that he thought they could sell 10,000 units

Morita sniffed and replied, "You will buy 50,000 initially, and 50,000 for second delivery." The New York office argued that "Walkman" was "Japanese language," and that the name would *never* be accepted in America. He convinced Morita to make the first 10,000 sets under the brand name Soundabout. In Sweden, the product was introduced as Freestyle, and in the United Kingdom as the Stowaway. In Canada, because we participated on the production line with SONY of America, the first 2,000 were also introduced as Soundabout.

When the product was shipped to America, the response was phenomenal. Instead of being discounted, as is usual in the electronics shops that abound in Manhattan, the price was raised by anywhere from 25 to 50 per cent; all stores were soon in a sold-out position. SONY had underestimated the demand, in spite of Morita's enthusiasm. Instead of a fad, a new niche was created in a world market that had never existed before.

Even SONY was astonished by the world-wide take off of the product, and they decided to advertise it under one name for all markets. The name Walkman was adopted, and it went on from success to success. Today, there are nearly two dozen different models, from the waterproof Walkman to portable CD players and more. The product has been shamelessly copied by every electronics manufacturer from Panasonic to Sanyo. But the SONY Walkman is the product in demand, and SONY has sold *tens of millions* of sets. Furthermore, Morita had the honour of creating a new English word. You will find "Walkman" listed in the Oxford Dictionary.

Together with other SONY products, such as broadcast equipment for the television industry, micro computers and word processors, the saga goes on. Sales increase year to year.

The Formation of the SONY Stores

On one of my many visits to Tokyo, I would often be invited to spend the evening at the Morita's home. On one such occasion I brought up the question of establishing a chain of SONY Stores in Canada. As SONY did not have any retail stores under their own name throughout the world, Morita asked me the reason for this suggestion. The year was 1981, when competition had become very keen in electronics with many well established names such as Toshiba, Hitachi, NEC, and Panasonic entering the Canadian and world markets that SONY had pioneered.

I pointed out that some department stores as well as independent retailers were *not* featuring SONY, as it was more in their interest to push the sale of their own brand names, which generated greater profit. They would use SONY, known for its quality, to advertise a lower price to bring the customer into their premises. Then the salesman, who worked on a percentage basis, would attempt to switch the customer to their own brand name because of the higher commission they would be paid on the sale.

"Won't this hurt our sales if we open stores to compete with our established sales outlets?" asked Morita.

"Not if we don't undersell our regular retail accounts" was my prompt reply.

I pointed out that we would carry the full line of SONY products. Our salesmen will be well trained to explain the products, which were becoming more and more complex each year. I told Akio that there was a small chain of retail stores in Vancouver named Miller's, which owed Gendis about $70,000. They were not paying their bills satisfactorily, and I had proposed buying the chain, which consisted of 12 stores located in Alberta and British Columbia. I proposed that these stores would be acquired by Gendis and operated as Miller SONY Stores. After a period of time, when my theory of operating our own stores was proven, we would drop the Miller name and then operate each as The SONY Store.

I suggested that it would be our intention to build a chain of at least 100 stores across Canada. It would be necessary, however, to experiment in the retail business, and because the Miller market was quite isolated from central Canada, it would not disturb our large accounts located there. Before we could expand the chain out of BC and Alberta, it was necessary to evolve a pattern and system that would work for us, so that when we decided to expand, we could do it quickly.

After some persuasion, Morita agreed, and I gave him my word that the chain, when proven successful, would be turned over to SONY for its assets. We shook hands and he agreed.

It was in May, 1981, during that same trip to Tokyo, that I stopped off in Vancouver to have a discussion with Del Miller, co-owner with his cousin, Albert Miller, of Miller Electronics Ltd. The small chain of stores was handling SONY products, as well as many other Japanese brands of electronics. Their purchases in the previous year would have been well over $800,000, from SONY, Vancouver branch, but their payments had been slow, as I would tell Akio Morita, and we were carrying them as a receivable for anywhere from three to four months.

Brother Joe was responsible in a large measure for Miller's being in the retail electronics business. Miller's was first and foremost a retail jeweler. In trying to develop new accounts, my brother Joe had persuaded Miller's to take on the SONY radios and tape recorders as a department in their jewellery stores. Del Miller had developed some background knowledge in electronics, because he foresaw the boom that was beginning in 1964 for audio hi-fi products. Miller's was so successful that it was not too long before Del opened the first Miller Electronics Store, which was financed by the jewellery chain.

Through the years, Miller's prospered, and by 1980 it was one of Vancouver's most prominent electronics chains. With the help of Joe, new stores were opened. In Edmonton, we made available a location on 101st, where there was a Metropolitan owned property. In Vancouver, Joe arranged for the property on Davie St. to be leased to Miller's. There was a certain amount of self interest in the help given Miller's, because every time a new store was opened, this meant an additional outlet for SONY products. There was a certain amount of loyalty generated between Miller's and SONY products. However, Miller's found that they had to handle competing lines like Pioneer, Sanyo and Toshiba, to maintain volume and remain competitive.

In conversation, Del Miller advised that he had options on opening three new stores to bring the chain up to fifteen. I told him that before I could make a definite commitment, I wished to explain to Mr. Akio Morita my intention to get SONY's approval for the purchase of the Miller chain.

There are many suppliers, Panasonic, Sanyo, Pioneer and JVC, among others–that all cater to the same account (in many towns there may be only one electronics retailer), and this puts the retailer in the position where he could make demands on the suppliers, and play one against another. By controlling our own retail chain, not only would Miller's carry the complete SONY line, but we would be able to intimate to an account that was not giving us fair representation that we were in a position to open a Miller's store in his area.

When the Miller acquisition was announced, we received inquiries from the press, and from some of our accounts, who wanted to know the reason for the move. I stated publicly, and it was reported in the press, that we had no intention of competing with our good SONY accounts. It was only in areas where SONY was under represented, that we would consider opening new Miller stores.

Surprisingly, the department stores welcomed this acquisition by Gendis. They felt that Miller's would now be more apt to adhere to list prices; in the past they had been notorious price-cutters. Many independent retailers lived on the verge of bankruptcy, and when they were pressed for payment of their accounts, they would resort to severe price-cutting on brand merchandise, to raise dollars, "robbing Peter to pay Paul." Now that Miller's was under control, we found better support from our major department stores in both provinces.

In analyzing the Miller acquisition, we found that they had written a number of poor leases, some of the stores were poorly located, they had many suppliers, and a record department that could not compete with the stores owned by the record companies. It was decided that, during fiscal year 1982, we would do a proper clean-up job.

We disposed of the record departments in all stores, taking substantial losses. We closed out all competing brand lines, such as Kenwood, Toshiba, Pioneer and TDK, as well as BASF and Maxell audio-tapes. We instructed Miller's to stock *only SONY products*, knowing full well that this was a dramatic change in their method of operation.

We closed two unprofitable stores, in one instance at no lease penalty, and in the other incurring a $30,000 pay-out. By sacrificing the products sold on a clean-out basis, the gross margin dropped dramatically, and we incurred a loss of approximately $2.6 million before tax.

We then went on a renovation program and spent about $1 million to bring the Miller operation up to the necessary SONY standard, adopting the name Miller, The SONY Store, to emphasize that Miller's was selling primarily SONY products. Using this logo left the possibility of such future additions to the chain as, Jones, The SONY Store. Eventually, the surname could be dropped, and across the country the chain would be known as The SONY Store.

Generations have grown up with the name SONY, after its decades in Canada, and the over $500 million in advertising spent in this country. Yet in a smaller community, where there might be only one retail electronics store, the salesperson might suggest another brand, and we failed to get the benefit of all our advertising. With our experimenting, we proved that we could go into an area that was under-represented in SONY products, open a store, sell SONY merchandise exclusively, and generate $1 million worth of sales in a twelve-month period.

The SONY Stores proved to be a success. In many cases, would-be customers came to the SONY Stores to see the full SONY line of products. The trained salesmen would explain the products to the full satisfaction of the customer, whether it resulted in a sale or not. No pressure for sales was made, as all salesmen were on fixed salaries. In many cases, a shopper, armed with the model number of the product he wished to buy, would make the purchase through a department store or an independent store that he preferred to trade with. The result was satisfactory either way, as it resulted in a SONY sale *wherever* the purchase was made.

By the mid-90s, in Canada alone, there were 77 SONY Stores which generated over one hundred million dollars in sales. SONY of Canada Ltd. was generating far more sales than any other electronic manufacturer.

By the year 2001 just ended; SONY sales in Canada generated sales of well over a billion dollars. Of this amount, the SONY stores were responsible for over 12% of these sales.

The Conclusion of The SONY Story

In the mid-90s, my formal, four-decade close relationship with SONY came to an end, when we sold our interest back to the SONY Corporation in Japan. In recalling those moments, I think back to how much impact General Distributors and SONY had upon one another.

Back in August, 1974, *Business Week* magazine quoted then-Prime Minister Trudeau as saying, "the Foreign Investment Review Agency, FIRA, take a hard line on any attempt to take over a Canadian company." This attitude by Ottawa came about just at the time when Gendis was discussing its joint venture with SONY, and it threw a roadblock into our negotiations.

Under the new FIRA regulations, even if Gendis would own 51% of the company, against 49% owned by SONY, the joint venture would be treated as a foreign company! When I questioned this during a trip to our nation's capital, I was told that, as long as SONY owned *any* percentage of the joint venture, our Winnipeg-headquartered, nation-wide company would still be considered foreign. Their reasoning was, SONY Corp. Tokyo would be controlling SONY of Canada Ltd., by being the supplier of the SONY product. Gendis was being treated as if they were the manufacturer by this legislation.

Nevertheless, we were still able to complete our joint venture in 1975, as I related earlier: 51% was owned by Gendis, 49% by SONY Tokyo, and, of the Gendis percentage, 2% were held in a voting trust. This joint venture, SONY of Canada Ltd., was managed by an equal number of directors from both Gendis and SONY Tokyo. When SONY achieved over 500 million dollars in sales, I began to hear warning bells ringing, which made me recall what happened when Pat Frawley sold out to Gillette, and did not protect our Canadian contract with Paper-Mate.

Up to that time, Akio Morita was still very much involved with SONY, and he and I were both aware of several major events which had occurred in over the previous decades, in which Gendis had a great influence on his company's early years: The first, of course, went back to our first meeting in Tokyo in 1955, when Gendis became the first to introduce and merchandise SONY products in Canada. As SONY's first export customer, our dealings gave Morita the momentum to influence Ibuka, that the proper direction for the future growth of their firm *was* through export.

The second important moment was when, in the early 1970s, I showed my profound trust in Morita and SONY by sending the $5-million transfer of funds without any note or any security on the part of SONY. I showed a deep trust that SONY would ship the merchandise that we had contracted for delivery, over the orders placed for six months' future delivery.

The third, of course, would be in the Deposition I would give on behalf of SONY, in 1978, when Universal and Disney took SONY to court to try and stop Betamax from coming to market. Morita became aware that I had correspondence with Taft Schreiber that would prove conclusively that Universal had been attempting through Gendis to acquire the Betamax product for their *own* purposes. There is no question that the Deposition held in Winnipeg proved that Universal did not have a case in trying to stop Betamax and VHS from marketing their products.

There was one proviso in the deal, which was crucial: After twenty years, SONY Tokyo had the right to exercise the 2% voting trust shares and, if they desired, an additional 15%. This way, they could gain control of SONY of Canada. If they chose to exercise those rights, that would leave Gendis as a minority shareholder, with 34% of the equity.

When we worked out this joint venture in 1975, I saw it as a necessity, in order to protect the interests of Gendis. We agreed to give up 100% of the profits we generated, by having the exclusive rights to market all SONY products. However, we did *not* participate in many of the new products which SONY kept bringing to the markets of the world. They held back some of these products from the Canadian market because they felt we lacked the personnel necessary to sell these new, sophisticated electronics in Canada.

But personal health can affect changes, even if friendships remain strong. Unfortunately, one by one, the founders of SONY Corporation began to vanish from the scene: Kazuo Iwama, Morita's brother-in-law, died in 1983. He was a fine gentleman and a close social friend. He had been given the task by Ibuka to develop the transistor, so that it could be used for radios and all the countless products that followed. During the next decade, Masaru Ibuka and Akio Morita, both suffered strokes, and were incapacitated. Masaru Ibuka died in 1998. Morita's cerebral hemorrhage occurred in late 1993 from which he really never recovered. He died in October 1999 at the age of 78.

True, Akio had spoken about our friendship and business relationship when he was honoured on May 29, 1987, with the International Distinguished Entrepreneur Award from the University of Manitoba: "As you know, SONY is an international company; we have operations all over the world. We have factories all over the world; we have operations all over the world. But the man who made our company an international company is my friend Albert Cohen. He was our first overseas customer, and this was our first export business. So that's why we owe Albert a great deal for his part in making us an international company."

I now found it necessary to negotiate with SONY's much younger executives, who were presently managing SONY. By 1995, international sales of its electronics products had reached $40-billion U.S., a huge number which would increase 50% by 2001, when SONY was listed among the 20 largest companies in the world. Understandably, the next generation of executives felt that Gendis had prospered over the years through this association with SONY.

Of the old guard, there was only Norio Ohga, who was aware of my early association with the founders of SONY. He was responsible for instructing Mickey Schuloff to make a deal with me to the satisfaction of both our companies.

In 1995, we sold our 51% interest to SONY Tokyo, after much bargaining, for $207-million, Canadian. This included the goodwill which was engendered over the many millions of dollars spent each year. All the real estate and the goodwill of SONY went back to Japan.

It was a smooth turnover, and it did not go unnoticed in the press. Ian G. Masters wrote, in *The Toronto Star,* on June 2, 1995: "The Japanese company has announced its intention of buying the shares of SONY of Canada that it doesn't now own. That may make sense, but it seems hard to imagine a SONY with neither a Morita nor a Cohen at the helm."

Norio Ohga was an enigma to most people who knew him. I had a few run-ins with him but we respected each other because we had the same interest in furthering the growth of SONY.

"No one addresses Mr. Morita as 'Akio'!" he told me on one occasion. *"I don't know what gives you the right to address him in such a manner! Why, I don't even call him by his first name, but rather, as Mr. Morita!"* This was on the occasion of one of our many meetings when I was spending many weeks in Japan in the early years.

"How long have you been with SONY?" I asked Ohga.

"Since 1970," he replied.

"Well, I was dealing with SONY *long* before *you* were here, and I respect Mr. Morita greatly. I usually address him as Mr. Morita when there are other people around. I took the liberty to refer to him as 'Akio' in front of you. He refers to me as 'Albert.' But since I don't know you that well, I call *you* 'Mr. Ohga'!"

My later confrontation with **Mr**. Ohga, was when Akio Morita had given me the okay to open the SONY Stores in Canada. The future CEO did not agree as to how these stores should be merchandised. I had to stand my ground against some of the advice he gave, and expected me to follow. Time proved me correct. The SONY Stores, a wholly-owned subsidiary of SONY of Canada Ltd., generated $120 million in 2001; in the same year, SONY of Canada Ltd. generated over $1.3 billion. In fact, perhaps if SONY U.S.A. had taken the Canadian lead in operating its own stores in the U.S.A., based on SONY Store sales in Canada, the equivalent in the United States could have generated over $1.2-billion U.S. in sales. This based on the fact that the Canadian population is 10% of the U.S.A.

Ohga's first love was music, and he was in Berlin after the war as a student of opera. Because of his musical career, he came across one of the first tape recorders in Japan manufactured by the young Totsuko company. Because of his fine ear, he wrote a letter to the small Japanese company strongly criticizing their recorder.

The letter made it to the desk of Akio Morita, who was interested by the criticism. He wrote Ohga, inviting him to meet with him and discuss some of the complaints he had. On his return to Japan, Ohga did impress Morita, who then brought in some engineers to hear the critique. Ohga returned to his studies in Berlin, while Morita incorporated Ohga's suggestions in the new products. Morita then asked Ohga to join the company, to which the young singer refused as he wanted to pursue his operatic career. It was only years later, when Akio was able to promise Ohga that, if he joined the company, he would be put in charge of their first venture with CBS Records. Two decades later, Norio Ohga was SONY's President and CEO!

Interestingly, it was a year after we sold our Canadian interest in SONY of Canada back to SONY Tokyo, that Norio Ohga invited me to attend the 50th anniversary celebrations of SONY Corporation in Japan. My son James, now on the Gendis board, joined me for the occasion, and we were warmly greeted by him. I appreciated the cordial reception which he had extended to James and myself, and believed that they now realized that the deal we had recently concluded was one which was fair to both partners.

Then, in a surprise move, Ohga decided to turn over the reins to his successor, Nobuyuki Idei, who now became Chairman and Chief Executive Officer. In turn, Idei appointed Kunitake Ando to the position of President and Chief Operating Officer. Although I knew the two new powerful heads of SONY Corporation, I had never had a close personal relationship with them, as I had with the three founding fathers of SONY.

One of the saddest events was when I was notified that on November 30th, 1993, Akio Morita suffered a cerebral hemorrhage. Morita was operated on the following day. The prognosis was that the chance of recovery was not too favourable but fortunately he was able to go on to a rehabilitation program.

Besides Dr. Akio Suzuki, Dean of the School of Medicine, there were other doctors Hirakawa, Ohno and Takada who assisted in the special attention and care while he convalesced.

I had the privilege as an old friend to visit Akio on two occasions. I would like to say that there could not be a more faithful and loving person than his wife Yoshiko. She, over the years of his convalescence, was with him day and night. As best as possible I know it assisted Akio in the years he survived until his passing on the 3rd of October, 1999.

I felt a personal loss. Japan, however, was the greatest loser on the passing of the man who became known as the personification of the new Japan.

I was pleasantly surprised to receive word, early in 2000, that Mr. Norio Ohga had proposed my name to the board of SONY Corporation of Japan: I was to be honoured as the first recipient of the SONY LIFETIME ACHIEVEMENT AWARD, which was presented in July 2000 at their annual meeting in Tokyo. There were over twelve hundred SONY executives from around the world who attended when this honour was conferred on me for which I felt truly grateful.

Even though by 1995 the profound, mutually-rewarding business and financial relationship between SONY of Japan and Gendis Inc. of Canada was over, the thousands of memories would go on.

Norio Ohga
Chairman
Chief Executive Officer

SONY

Sony Corporation
6-7-35, Kitashinagawa
Shinagawa-ku, Tokyo, 141 Japan
Telephone: (03) 5448-2450
Fax: (03) 5448-4250

January 21, 1998

Mr. Albert D. Cohen
Chairman & CEO
Gendis Inc.
1370 Sony Place
Winnipeg MB R3C 3C3

Dear *Albert*

Thank you for your letter of January 7th together with the copies of the Proforma Invoices. What a big surprise and a great pleasure to see such historical papers after just celebrating the 50th year of our company! Gendis is probably the only company that possess such precious papers from the old days when our company was still called the Tokyo Tsushin Kogyo.

Incidentally, January 26th happens to be Mr. Morita's seventy-seventh birthday, and I would like to show the copies to him on that occasion. I am sure that he will be very happy to see the papers. It will remind him of the time when he first expanded his dreams overseas with your cooperation.

Wishing you all the best in your endeavors and I hope to see you again in the near future..

Sincerely yours,

Norio Ohga

NO/ya

Some Final Reminiscences

One could claim that my career truly began in 1939, when General Distributors was founded, but that might be too limiting - even if that event **is** already 63 years in the past! I learned so very much about merchandising years before we formed our first, formal company. A psychologist might suggest that the inspiration which drove me to seek out Paper-Mate, find and befriend Akio Morita and the future SONY empire, create SAAN stores, purchase Metropolitan, Greenbergs, and go into drilling for oil, could be traced back to my childhood - the longing to succeed and "make it" in the New World. This was first shown by my grandfather, an immigrant in a land that was strange to him and his family who arrived in the Canadian west with not much more than a hope to succeed.

The day when Akio handed me a blank little metal disk and told me, "Albert, look at this: it is going to change the entire record business, and will make 8-tracks and even LPs obsolete!" It was, of course, one of the first compact discs, or CDs. Morita, to show its potential, had ordered his engineers to create a CD with the capability to record *all* of Beethoven's Ninth Symphony, "The Choral" on a single CD.

Looking back it is amazing that a little Japanese factory named Totsuko in 1955, later known as SONY, would affect the future of consumer electronics throughout the world.

One of the few trips that Akio Morita made to Canada, someone asked him, "Why do you not visit this country more often?" To which Morita replied, **"I am a trouble shooter, but I *never* have any trouble to shoot in Canada!"**

When Chauvco sold the company to Pioneer Resources, Guy Turcotte did not include Chauvco's interest in what was to become the largest pipeline in North America, namely the Alliance Pipeline. When we had the opportunity to become the largest single shareholder in Fort Chicago which held approximately 26% interest in the Alliance Pipeline, the banks were quickly on-side, ready to loan us the tens of millions we needed to invest in that great new project. And since the shares of Fort Chicago have now risen from $5.75 to over $9 on the Toronto Stock Exchange, this became one more example of how keeping one's good name can mean future success, as well as self-respect.

If the six brothers had not worked toward the same goal, this book would be much thinner. In the early years of General Distributors, our success could not have happened without the cooperation of all six of us. True, I discovered the products and purchased them, but they each had connections in their respective cities, and they each contributed to the success of Gendis Inc.

I had made it clear to each of my brothers: *"Any time you want to have a new President, all you have to do is get three brothers to agree to this, and I'll be the **fourth** vote. I'd vote with them, so you could easily make a change in leadership."* They never did and they often showed their appreciation for my "discovery" of Paper-Mate and SONY.

I was simply trying to build a successful business, and my five brothers were all part of it. And the eventual success could *not* have occurred without them. Of course, once we took the company public - one of the smartest things I ever did - there could not be any arguments.

This may be the place to refer to a rather fascinating friendship which I had with a very famous writer over several decades: Ian Fleming, the author of the widely-read James Bond series. It was back in 1959 when I first met Ian Fleming. It seemed like merely a casual encounter, which showed no promise of developing further.

As one might expect, our conversations eventually turned to business, and in September 1961, I received a letter from Fleming: "I was much interested in hearing your tale of Metropolitan Stores," he wrote me. "It looks like an immensely exciting affair, and with you as chairman I am sure it will be a most profitable venture. Please let me know if you advise me to make a modest investment in shares."

Soon after, Fleming - now a wealthy author and growing more successful every day - actually became a shareholder in Metropolitan shares. Whether this influenced him very much in the adventures he was continually inventing for his hero, James Bond, I am not sure. But he did choose to create a heroine from Canada in **The Spy Who Loved Me**, about which he wrote to me, "I think Canadian book shops have been a bit leery of it as I have some rather spikey things to say about Quebec."

In 1963 the two of us had our own respective special events. Gendis was opening a new SONY office and warehouse building in Montreal and Ian's **From Russia With Love** was opening in London. It was then the author wittily wrote to me, "It is indeed extraordinary the amount of publicity this fellow James Bond and I are getting all over the place. Although it's good for business, to tell you the truth, I would be very glad to pass some of it on to the Metropolitan Stores. I see your shares are on the move. Good show!"

I mention the above friendship for a reason. In a conversation last year, I mentioned to the President of SONY Corporation of America, Howard Stringer, that Fleming and I had been good friends, and that he had autographed a first edition of his book as a gift. Howard suggested that there were fan clubs in England that were collectors of Ian Fleming mementos.

I had my personal secretary Terry Smitzniuk contact Christie's of England to see if they were interested to sell our correspondence, along with several of Fleming's adventure novels, including **Casino Royale, From Russia With Love,** and **Doctor No.** I wondered if there could be a market for letters between Fleming and myself which declared such personal things as: "The maddening thing is that I was in Japan between 14th and 29th November, and though I was traveling a secret route in pursuit of James Bond way down south, it crossed my mind from time to time to ring up SONY and see if by chance you were in the country. . . ."

I had no idea what this memorabilia would be worth, and was completely taken aback to hear that the lot went for *over six thousand Pounds Sterling!* And so, the proceeds received from the sale of the Ian Fleming material were donated, "in the memory of Ian Fleming," to the Winnipeg Health Sciences Centre Foundation ($3,000), the St. Boniface General Hospital Research Foundation ($3,000), the Victoria General Hospital Foundation, ($3,000), and the Winnipeg Free Press Christmas Cheer Board ($1,000).

In a small way, the character of James Bond and the man who created him, not only continues to stop nuclear wars and strike down evildoers, but also assisted some very worthwhile causes in faraway Winnipeg.

It was after our harrowing experience when we were ordered out of Prague that I wrote to Fleming from Paris. I told him in my letter of the narrow escape and that Irena and I would be at the Savoy Hotel in London before returning to Canada.

To my surprise, Ian called me the day of our arrival and invited us to join him for dinner at his place. He was going to send his car for us. When I related to Irena that she was going to meet a very interesting person, she said, "What about Anthony?" I replied that that they have very good babysitters that the Savoy would arrange for the evening. Irena, however, was still concerned that even in London she would not let Anthony alone.

When I called Ian and told him of Irena's concern he said he was sending his car and bring Anthony along. When we arrived, Ian opened his son's room with many toys to keep Anthony happy.

When I related our events that took place in Prague he shook his head and said, "You know you put your head in the lion's mouth and you were lucky to get out." And so we spent a most enjoyable evening with Ian Fleming. It was just about the time when he was achieving world fame for his James Bond character.

Some of our correspondence is of interest which gives the idea of this most modest man who accepted his fame with true modesty.

As for Ted Arcand who had been of great help in assisting our exit from the then communist Czechoslovakia, we kept in touch over the years. He went on to become Ambassador to the Emirate States then Ambassador to Hungary and finally Ambassador to the Holy See in Rome.

Ted Arcand is now retired and not too long ago we met in Ottawa. Over drinks we both caught up with events that followed our adventure in Prague.

4, Old Mitre Court,
Fleet Street, E.C.4.
Ludgate Circus 8655.

14th September, 1961

My dear Albert,

Thank you a thousand times for your
charming present. What wonderful little machines
these are, I almost feel inclined to listen to the
damn thing myself!

I was also much interested in hearing
your tale of Metropolitan Stores and reading the
prospectus. It looks an immensely exciting affair,
and with you as Chairman I am sure will be a most
profitable venture.

Please let me know if you advise me to
make a modest investment in the shares.

It was such fun seeing you all on Monday.
What a beautiful girl your wife is, and it was
wonderful to see how much Anthony has inherited
both of your good looks.

Please continue to keep in touch.

Yours ever
Ian

Albert D. Cohen Esq.,
305, Park Boulevard,
Tuxedo,
Manitoba, Canada

4, Old Mitre Court,
Fleet Street, E.C.4.
Ludgate Circus 8655.

17th April, 1962

My dear Albert,

Thank you very much for your charming letter from Nassau which, for some unknown reason, has only just arrived.   Presumably you sent it by carrier pigeon!

It is all most annoying because I was in Nassau from 14th to the 16th of March on my way back from Jamaica and we could have met if we had been equipped with second sight.

The new book, called The Spy Who Loved Me, is out in America and here, but I think the Canadian book shops have been a bit leary of it as I have some rather spikey things to say about Quebec!

Thanks to plenty of nicotine and alcohol I am keeping fit enough and have just finished an immensely long James Bond story for next year.

What you say about Metropolitan is most encouraging. My investments are run by Robert Fleming and Company, my family merchant bank, and I have asked them if they approve, to make an investment for both Anne and me.   So from now on I hope you will be working for me as diligently as I write for you!

Anyway thank you very much for your advice about the Company.

Come over again soon and anyway we will try and meet when the family comes over in the summer.

With best wishes to the family,

Yours ever,

Ian

Albert D. Cohen Esq.,
305, Park Boulevard,
Tuxedo, Manitoba,
Canada

4, Old Mitre Court,
Fleet Street, E.C.4.
Ludgate Circus 8655.

5th December, 1962

My dear Albert,

It was a tremendous excitement and surprise to receive this cheerful homunculus, so
beautifully carved, from you in Japan.

Let us hope it inspires me to further
labours on your behalf.

The maddening thing is that I was in
Japan between 14th and 29th November, and though
I was travelling a secret route in pursuit of James
Bond way down south, it crossed my mind from time
to time to ring up Sony and see if by chance you
were in the country.

But it seemed so unlikely and I was so
desperately on the move that I did nothing about it.

It just shows that one should follow one's
intuition.

Anyway thank you a thousand times again for
thinking of me from time to time as I do of you.

With affectionate wishes to you all for
Christmas,

Yours ever,

Ian.

Albert D. Cohen Esq.,
Chairman, Metropolitan Stores,
305, Park Boulevard, Tuxedo,
Manitoba, Canada.

4, Old Mitre Court,
Fleet Street, E.C.4.
Ludgate Circus 8655.

9th October, 1963

My dear Albert,

It was very nice indeed to hear from you
and, as you can guess, I'm afraid I shan't be able
to come to your opening on November 7th any more
than you will be able to come to my first night
of "From Russia, With Love" in London tomorrow
night.

It is indeed extraordinary the amount of
publicity I and this fellow James Bond are getting
all over the place. Although it's good for business, to tell you the truth I would be very glad to
pass some of it on to Metropolitan Stores!

I was very glad to hear all your news and
I only wish I could get away from here and do some
of this travelling with you.

It's very satisfactory that you now have all
the family together, and of course if you do get down
to Jamaica I shall look forward enormously to seeing
you and Irena.   I expect to be there from January 15th
for about two months at Goldeneye, Oracabessa, and my
telephone number is in the book.

I see your shares are on the move.   Good
show!

With my very best wishes to you both.

Yours ever

Ian.

Albert D. Cohen Esq.,
General Distributors Ltd.,
791, Notre Dame Avenue,
Winnipeg, 3.

A Final Thought or Two

When my first book was published in 1985, the respected University of Toronto historian and prolific author Michael Bliss wrote a very generous review. When I came across it in my files the other day, some of the words made me realize where the Story of Six Brothers and Their Dream might actually fit into Canadian business history - a land which gave my parents and grandparents a place to sink roots and thrive.

> The Left claims that monopolistic corporations are everything, that the rich get richer and there are no more opportunities for the hard working and the ambitious. Along come people like the Cohens in every generation to prove how completely the critics misunderstand the dynamism of our enterprise system.
>
> To an historian, it is an intriguing story of the rise of a new transoceanic trading connection. As they import shiploads of Sony TVs, VCRs and other products for distribution across Canada, the Cohens are following in the footsteps of the great Montreal merchants of 150 years ago, who supplied the Canadas with the dry goods and hardware of England and Europe. The merchant princes of the old international trading system were then eclipsed by manufacturers, financiers and railway builders, but their importance is growing again in our re-internationalized economic world.
>
> Michael Bliss

That's kind, and maybe a bit generous. In other ways, the story of Gendis Inc. is also a story of the love and trust of a family - a mother, a father, and their six sons. And, of course, the love, trust, and abiding friendship between two young men - one from Canada, the other from faraway Japan.

In concluding this history of the company, which is autobiographical to some extent, I realize that the story is far from finished. This history has recorded events as they happened, to the best of my recollection. Memories do grow dim, and events often are exaggerated in their telling. Fortunately, through personal files, many of the events, anecdotes and happenings are backed by letters, newspaper clippings and other documentation to substantiate the facts.

There have been many highlights in the rather eventful history of Gendis Inc., born General Distributors. Paper-Mate certainly gave us visibility and the first chance to become a national company but it was never a huge profit-maker. It was SONY, of course, that made us international. Without that inspired firm, and its amazing products, there is no way that we could have gone public.

Sometimes I think that I must have some Japanese blood in me. One of the reasons why I got along so well with Morita was that he could see that I understood his motivation. I told him on day one that I would rather pay more money for his merchandise; I wanted him to build quality. If we were to advertise a product, we were not looking for a profit today. We were looking to invest in a new company but could not anticipate the future growth of what was to become the world famous SONY Corporation.

Once, on a golf course with Morita, I joked with him that I was in the Canadian Navy and he was in the Japanese Navy. I was in Halifax Harbour; he was in Japanese Bay. "It's a good thing we never met back then," I laughed, "or we might not be doing business together today!" Indeed, if it were businessmen dealing with world affairs, I don't think we'd have wars. Maybe trade wars, but not violent ones.

On the celebration of SONY of Canada's 30th anniversary in Toronto, I presented a plaque to Morita inscribed with a haiku verse I had written for me in Japanese, which in the Kanji form said:

>*Enkaku no chini arishi*
>*Nisha no deaiwa*
>*Ono Ono no chini*
>*Igyo wo*
>*Jyojyu seshimeta*
>*Korewa unmei teki*
>*Kaikou to ieyo*

The translation reads:

>*From opposite ends of the world we met*
>*Two great enterprises were born*
>*Did we make it happen - Or was it fate?*

I would like to end this saga with these two elegies. From time to time as most of you who will have read the chapters of "The Triangle of Success – The Gendis / SAAN Story", there is so much wisdom in both Jonathon Swift's "Satyrical Elegy" and the wisdom of "The Grass is Greener". Jonathan Swift wrote the following on the death of the Duke of Marlborough in 1722:

A Satyrical Elegy on the Death of a Late Famous General

His Grace! impossible! what, dead!
Of old age, too, and in his bed!
And could that mighty warrior fall,
And so inglorious, after all?
Well, since he's gone, no matter how,
The last loud trump must wake him now;
And, trust me, as the noise grows stronger,
He'd wish to sleep a little longer.
And could he be indeed so old
As by the newspapers we're told?
Threescore, I think, is pretty high;
'Twas time, in conscience he should die!
This world he cumber'd long enough;
He burnt his candle to the snuff;
And that's the reason, some folks think,
He left behind so great a stink.
Behold his funeral appears,
Nor widow's sighs, nor orphan's tears.
Wont at such times each heart to pierce,
Attend the progress of his hearse.
And what of that? his friends may say,
He had those honours in his day.
True to his profit and his pride,
He made them weep before he died.
Come hither, all ye empty things,
Ye bubbles raised by breath of kings!
Who float upon the tide of state;
Come hither, and behold your fate.
Let Pride be taught by this rebuke.
How every mean a thing's a duke;
From all his ill-got honours flung,
Turn'd to that dirt from whence he sprung.

The grass is always greener ... Upon the other side.
The thing that's most attractive is ... The one we haven't tried.
The single would be married ... The married would be free.
The worker, an executive... The boss, an employee.
The child would be an adult ... The man, a child again.
The rich would live a simple life... The poor, exchange with them.
And I, I would be what I am ... Just that and nothing more.
Except a brighter, richer man... And younger by a score.

In closing this volume, which took years of research and dedication to bring to fruition, there is a great feeling of personal satisfaction. The prime purpose of the exercise was to leave a history of how A. Cohen and Son grew from the summer of 1931 into Gendis Inc., the name the company bears today. The torch will be passed to continue the passage of time in the saga of Gendis Inc. To those who will follow, the challenge remains to keep the company on track to future success and to remember that this all happened in a true, ancient tradition:

A HANDSHAKE IS A SEAL
MORE WORTHY THAN ANY LEGAL DOCUMENT